Psychotherapy With Borderline Patients

An Integrated Approach

Psychotherapy With Borderline Patients

An Integrated Approach

David M. Allen
University of Tennessee

LEA

LAWRENCE ERLBAUM ASSOCIATES, PUBLISHERS

2003   Mahwah, New Jersey   London

Lawrence Erlbaum Associates, Inc., Publishers
10 Industrial Avenue
Mahwah, NJ 07430

Cover design by Kathryn Houghtaling Lacey

Library of Congress Cataloging-in-Publication Data

Allen, David M., 1949
Psychotherapy with borderline patients: An integrated approach /
    David M. Allen
        p. cm.
    Includes bibliographical references and index.
    ISBN 0-8058-4272-1 (cloth : alk. paper)
    1. Borderline personality disorder—Treatment. 2. Psychotherapy.
    I. Title. [DNLM: 1. Borderline personality Disorder—therapy.
    2. Psychotherapy—methods. 3. Family relations. WM 190 A425i
    2002]
RC569.5.B67 A45   2002
616.85′8520651 —dc21   2002067076
                                                              CIP

Printed in the United States of America
10 9 8 7 6 5 4 3 2 1

Contents

Preface

The broad range of symptoms, dysfunctional interpersonal interactions, provocative behavior in therapy, and comorbid psychiatric disturbances exhibited by patients with borderline personality disorder (BPD) make the disorder a model for the study of all forms of self-destructive and self-defeating behavior patterns. BPD has been termed by some the personality disorder without a specialty, and indeed may represent a measure of overall personality disturbance rather than a disorder unto itself (Livesay, 2000). In addition, the heterogeneous manifestations of the disorder represent a microcosm of the theoretical and practical issues that have come to dominate debates within the field of psychotherapy and psychiatric treatment. The nature–nurture debate, termed solved by some, is alive and well in discussions by practitioners of different theoretical bents about the genesis and phenomenology of BPD. Different aspects of the disorder cut across a broad span of issues with which almost all practicing clinicians in the behavioral health field must wrestle.

In my own efforts at treating this common and exceedingly frustrating disorder by applying different therapy paradigms, the current and ongoing behavior of the patient's family of origin began to appear to be by far the most important factor in reinforcing the patient's dysfunctional interpersonal behavior. The interpersonal behavior, it further seemed, was at the root of many if not most of the other manifestations of BPD. The attempt to integrate various approaches with this in mind led me to the development of *Unified Therapy* (Allen, 1988, 1991, 1993), a general treatment method for treating most forms of self-destructive or self-defeating behavior patterns. This book focuses more specifically on the treatment of BPD.

It describes a treatment method for adults with the disorder that specifically addresses major ongoing family dysfunction that presents in the here and now. The idea that disturbed and dysfunctional behavior within the patient's family of origin plays a role in BPD is widely acknowledged. However, its nature, causes, time frame, and salience as a factor creating and maintaining the disorder remain controversial. *Psychotherapy With Borderline Patients: An Integrated Approach* attempts to address this controversy.

It is meant for psychotherapists trained in all disciplines who treat patients with the full personality disorder, borderline traits, or other forms of self-destructive or self-defeating behavior. It integrates ideas and techniques from biological, family systems, psychodynamic, and cognitive-behavioral treatments in order to provide a treatment manual for individual psychotherapy with adults having these problems. It is as problem-focused and clinically oriented as I could make it. Although it contains theoretical material about borderline family dynamics—the understanding of which is necessary for the therapist to employ the recommended therapy techniques—it is primarily devoted to concrete treatment recommendations as well as practical solutions for commonly encountered problem patient behavior and symptoms.

The data on which this book's theory and treatment method are based come primarily from a series of detailed clinical case studies. For the past 20 years I have been observing and collecting data about the interactions of my patients with BPD and their parents. In addition to detailed and extensive descriptions of family interactions and genogram data collected from a wide variety of patients, I have used conjoint sessions, recordings of telephone conversations between patients with BPD and a parent, and written communication between them for this purpose. I have seen several parents of progeny with the disorder by themselves in individual psychotherapy. In my capacity as residency training director in the Department of Psychiatry at the University of Tennessee, I have collected videotapes of both individual and family therapy sessions of BPD patients with trainees. In a few instances, a parent of a BPD patient has been in therapy with one of my trainees at the same time as the BPD offspring was in therapy with a different one. The descriptions by the patient and the parent of the very same interactions from their different perspectives were compared and analyzed. We have also been collecting some outcome data for the treatment. My hope is that this book will spur others to study treatments aimed at present day interactions of adults with BPD and members of their families of origin.

The book is organized into two parts. The first part provides an understanding of the role of family in the genesis and maintenance of the disorder as well as clinical examples of family histories and family communication patterns. Chapter 1 reviews the literature on family interactions in patients with borderline disorders. It describes the characteristic oscillating pattern of hostile over- and underinvolvement between adults with the disorder and those who had served as primary caretakers for them when they were children. Chapter 2 describes the scientific underpinnings of the family dysfunction from the biological, sociological, and cognitive perspectives. It introduces the family systems role of the "spoiler" and examines its nature, manifestations, and origin. It goes on to elucidate reasons for the multiplicity of presentations characteristic of the disorder as well as for the presence or absence of comorbid personality disturbances. Chapter 3 proposes reasons for the unusual behavior observed in the parents of patients with the disorder, and presents a model for understanding its manifestations and its origin within a three-generational history of the family. Clinical examples of genogram material from the families of patients are provided. Chapter 4 is devoted to the nature of dysfunctional communication patterns in the families of BPD patients as well as to a description of how family members come to misunderstand one another.

Part 2 consists of the treatment manual. Chapter 5 presents an overview of the approach and provides its rationale and basic premises. It addresses controversies about the book's models for both the genesis and treatment of the disorder. Chapter 6 is devoted to techniques for managing the acting out of the patient with BPD within the transference relationship with the therapist, so that the real work of systems-oriented therapy can proceed. Chapter 7 describes an approach to the initial evaluation of patients with the disorder and discusses the use of medication and other symptomatic treatments for such problems as depression, anxiety, and self-mutilation. Suggestions are provided for getting around the dilemma of treatment limitations from managed care insurance companies. Chapter 8 describes ways to avoid being misled by the so-called "distortions" of the patient with BPD and suggests methods for demonstrating to patients the link between their symptomatology and specific patterns of family dysfunction. In addition, a protocol for conjoint sessions with other family members is described. Chapter 9 elucidates the development of strategies so that the patient can begin problem-solving communication with family members about dysfunctional interactions that trigger or reinforce self-destructive acting out. Specific techniques by which role-playing is used to design and practice these strategies are described in detail. The last chapter is devoted to termination issues including so-called postindividuation depression and family relapses.

By way of acknowledgment, I thank my colleagues Richard Farmer, M.D. and Hillel Abramson, PhD. They have helped me begin to collect empirical data on both the theory of personality pathology described in this book and outcomes of the treatment approach. I would like to thank the psychiatry residents and psychology interns who have helped me collect videotapes of patients with the borderline diagnosis interacting with their family members or describing their family relationships. Last I thank all of the patients I have seen in therapy who have patiently allowed me to gather extensive information about the interpersonal interactional patterns within their families, as well as the stories about how their families developed these patterns over three or more generations.

I

The Relationship Between
Family of Origin
and Individual Dynamics
of Adults With Borderline
Personality Disorder

1

The Borderline Family

The relationship between ongoing interpersonal interactions within the family of origin of adult patients with borderline personality disorder (BPD) and the patient's symptoms and behavior patterns is a critical one. An understanding of this relationship opens up new strategies for successful psychotherapy with these patients. The aim of this book is to explicate this relationship and to describe in detail a method of psychotherapy based on this understanding. We look at the nature and interpersonal causes of behavior patterns of patients with BPD, as well as treatment techniques for changing them, from a perspective that integrates family systems, psychodynamic, and cognitive-behavioral ideas.

Almost all theoretical concepts of BPD acknowledge the effects of experiences within the family of origin on the genesis of certain aspects of the disorder (Allen & Farmer, 1996). Even biogenetic hypotheses presuppose an interaction between a vulnerable central nervous system and environmental traumata (Paris, 1993; Van Reekum, 1993). Some authors have compared BPD to posttraumatic stress disorder, postulating a relationship between the disorder and physical or sexual abuse within the family (Gunderson & Sabo, 1993). Such abuse is reported to be present in the past history of a significant proportion of patients with BPD (Herman, Perry, & van der Kolk, 1989; Ogata et al., 1990; Zanarini, Gunderson, Marino, Schwartz, & Frankenburg, 1989). Linehan's (1993) highly regarded

*Portions of this chapter previously appeared in Allen & Farmer, 1996, and Allen, 2001.

theory of dialectical behavior therapy postulates that one of the major causative factors of BPD is an "invalidating environment," defined as one in which communication of private experiences is met by erratic, inappropriate, or extreme responses. That environment is almost invariably the family environment.

Because the therapists who first described BPD were primarily psychoanalysts, and because of the analytic view that early childhood experiences are the primary source of adult psychopathology, very little has been written about the family interactions of adult patients with the disorder. The clinical and theoretical literature about family of origin interactions of adult patients with BPD consists mostly of retrospective reports about those interactions that occurred during their early childhood or, to a lesser extent, their adolescence. In the extensive clinical experience of the author, these troublesome interactions and their importance in the pathogenesis of BPD behavior and symptomatology do not cease after a child grows up or leaves home. They continue well into the patient's adult life.

One of the basic premises on which the treatment method described in this book is based is as follows: Certain ongoing, present-day, transactional patterns among such individuals and members of their family of origin influence, trigger, and maintain the troublesome affects, cognitions, and behavior that make the patient suffering with the disorder so miserable and so difficult to treat. Before discussing in detail how and why this process plays out, I first briefly review some of the current literature about the family experiences of patients with the disorder.

FAMILY EXPERIENCES OF BPD PATIENTS: CURRENT PERSPECTIVES

The prevalent psychoanalytic view regarding the genesis of BPD behavior is that the family environment has a toxic effect on the development of the young child, which then leads to a developmental arrest (Masterson, 1981). However, several authors suggest that, although experiences at each developmental stage are important in personality formation, longer-term continuous experiences are also relevant to the genesis of adult personality disorders (Links & Munroe-Blum, 1990; Paris, 1993). According to this view, problematic family patterns expose vulnerable children to chronic rather than episodic stress and abuse, which results in continuous development of problematic behavior patterns. These patterns are then acted out in later life.

Zanarini and Frankenburg (1994) hypothesized that borderline psychopathology develops "in response to serious, chronic maladaptive behaviors on the part of immature and emotionally incompetent, but not necessarily deliberately malevolent, caregivers" (p. 26). Consistent with this view, Millon (1987) observed that "the significance of early troubled relationships may inhere less in their singularity or the depth of their impact than in the fact that they are precursors of what is likely to become a recurrent pattern of subsequent parental encounters" (p. 360). He added, "Early learnings fail to change, therefore, not because they have jelled permanently but because the same slender band of experiences which helped form them initially continue and persist as influences for years" (p. 361).

Links and Monroe-Blum (1990) reviewed 10 studies on the childhood environments of patients with BPD (Akiskal et al., 1985; Bradley, 1979; Frank & Paris, 1981; Goldberg, Mann, Wise, & Segall, 1985; Gunderson, Kerr, & Englund, 1980; Herman, Perry, & van der Kolk, 1989; Links, Steiner, & Offord, 1988; Snyder, Pitts, Goodpaster, & Gustin, 1984; Soloff & Millward, 1983; Zanarini et al., 1989). As the studies are all based on potentially biased retrospective patient reports, the results must be interpreted with some caution. Nonetheless, the fact that several themes recur time and time again lends some credence to their validity. Additionally, these conclusions have been replicated several times in later studies. These themes include family histories of neglect, abuse, loss, overprotection, overinvolvement, and *biparental failure*. Biparental failure is defined as a significant impairment in both parents that leads to a failure to carry out parental functions.

Although superficially somewhat dissimilar, these themes can be conceptualized in an integrated way. All of them relate to the polarized manner in which these parents are involved with their children. The themes reflect either the parents' persistent overinvolvement or persistent underinvolvement with their child. Incest, for example, may be thought of as extreme, inappropriate overinvolvement of, say, a father with his own daughter.

Walsh (1977) first suggested the idea that a combination of *both* parental overinvolvement *and* underinvolvement might be present in these families, rather than just one or the other. Melges and Swartz (1989) described oscillations in attachment behavior in patients with borderline personality between the two extremes. They postulate that these oscillations stem from patients' fears that they will be abandoned if they grow up and become independent of their families, but dominated and controlled if they remain close. These authors believe that, consistent with attachment theory, this pattern emerges from ambivalent reactions to children by their caretakers. A prospective study of family interactions and the emergence of BPD (Bezirganian, Cohen, & Brook, 1993) is consistent with these formulations. They find that neither maternal overinvolvement nor maternal inconsistency alone predicts emergence of BPD, but the coexistence of the two factors together does.

The paradigm of Melges and Schwartz (1989) described earlier receives further empirical support from the work of Shapiro (1978, 1982, 1992) and Shapiro and Freedman (1987). The latter authors base their findings on extensive observations of the families of adolescents diagnosed with BPD. They find that, in the families of patients with BPD, both parents seemed to experience major conflicts regarding the issue of their child's autonomy. The conflicts seem to prevent them from responding to their adolescent's growing independence in appropriate ways. A common pattern is that the parents experience their child as clinging and demanding, and become angry about it. This results in the parents' defensive withdrawal from their teen. However, even while neglecting the developing needs of the adolescent, the parents continue to focus much of their attention on the child.

Similar patterns have been observed in the case material described by interpersonal theorists and researchers. Benjamin (1993) described an interpersonal theory of borderline behavior patterns. She viewed the behavior of the patient with BPD as a response to other people, primarily those within the patient's family of origin and spousal relationships. She observed that the family backgrounds of individuals with borderline traits show four major characteristics:

1. Family chaos in which the individual with BPD is subtly blamed for family problems and is expected to exert control over family misbehavior.

2. Episodes of traumatic abandonment (such as being locked in a closet) interspersed with periods of traumatic overinvolvement (such as an incestual assault).
3. Efforts by the individual with BPD to establish autonomy that are interpreted by the family as disloyal.
4. Parental love and concern that are elicited only when the patient presents with misery, sickness, and debilitation.

Patterns like these are likely to be ingrained characteristics of the dysfunctional interactions within these families. As such, it would seem unlikely that they would dissipate as the children in the family mature into adult life. In the next section, I present some examples of ongoing family patterns that I believe to be major factors in the genesis and maintenance of BPD symptoms and behavior patterns.

FAMILY INTERACTIONS OF ADULTS
WITH BORDERLINE PERSONALITY DISORDER

I initially became interested in the family dynamics of adult patients with BPD after a particularly dramatic incident during my treatment of a hospitalized young woman. This rather rude introduction took place during my first year in private psychiatric practice. Having had very little family therapy training during my psychiatric residency training, and being young and green in more ways than one, I was completely unprepared for what was to come.

A 21-year-old woman (Case I-A) was referred to me for psychiatric hospitalization because of ongoing violent episodes that took place in her mother's home, wherein the patient resided. To my knowledge, all of this violence had been directed toward inanimate objects. I was told that she had, at several different times during temper outbursts, destroyed pieces of furniture and other objects. When we first met, the girl, who was quite strong, was taking exception to being admitted into a psychiatric inpatient ward. She was thrashing about so aggressively that it took three large male psychiatric technicians to restrain her.

After she had calmed down, and despite my having little family training, I decided to meet with both the patient and her mother. Much later on, I had the opportunity to see the patient's mother and a sibling alone in individual psychotherapy. Additionally, I had conjoint sessions with her and her father. These sessions gave me a good opportunity to get a pretty good picture of one "borderline" family.

The mother, it later turned out, had the disorder herself, as did several other family members. It is believed that many of the parents of borderlines also suffer from the disorder; it may be true, in fact, that there are first-generation borderlines and second-generation borderlines who are somewhat different. I have observed that it is in the nature of borderline psychodynamics to reproduce themselves.

During my first session with the patient and her mother, both of them complained bitterly about one another. Mom complained that the daughter continuously dropped classes at college on various pretexts, and picked fights with school officials. She complained about the patient's occasional drug use, and opined that perhaps the patient had become brain damaged. She wondered aloud why the patient's anger always seemed to focus on her and never on the patient's father. After all, her ex-husband had spent little time with her and had never paid nor even offered child support. Oddly, the mother then volunteered that she had never pursued the patient's father for back child support. In fact, she had run up huge charge bills and then sat around and waited for the ex-husband to pay them. Of course, he never did.

The patient countercomplained that the mother did not have any money to help her buy books and pay college fees. Furthermore, although her mother had given her the "gift" of a car to get to college, the car did not run. She stated that her mother would complain about her not having applied for financial aid, but would not fill out the forms the patient had given her for that very purpose.

The conjoint session quickly began to deteriorate at an alarming rate. The mother suggested to the patient that she go to school full time—or maybe she should drop out altogether in order to get her head straight. At that point, the subject suddenly seemed to change completely. The patient started to complain that the two of them lived like pigs, because the mother would come home from work, do nothing but sit around watching television and eating, and leave a huge mess. The mother responded that her habits were none of the daughter's business. The daughter replied that maybe she should just leave, and insisted that the she could go out and support herself, without any help from the mother. Mother then said, "But you'll support yourself by selling drugs!" Mother then added, "I found your drugs and flushed them down the toilet."

Suddenly and without warning, the patient went into a rage. In response, the mother, instead of moving back prudently, put her nose in the patient's face and began berating her daughter. Before I had the slightest chance to try to intervene, the patient slammed her closed fist into the mother's face with as much force as she could muster. The technicians quickly came and dragged her away.

What impressed me the most about all this, other than the fact that at that time I had not a clue as to the nuances of the argument they were having, was not the violent behavior of daughter. The mother's behavior was far more fascinating. I had barely met the patient and I had already been informed that the daughter was violent. Obviously, Mom knew this better than anyone. She was not stupid; she'd witnessed the rage first-hand. Granted, the patient had supposedly not hit anyone before, but why on earth would the mother stick her nose in the patient's face in the middle of the rage? A lay person might say, only half in jest, that mom was "asking for it."

Since this episode, I have continued to notice similar peculiar behavior in the parents of adults with BPD. I am not alone in this observation; many other writers from all therapy schools have commented about this as well. For example, the analytically oriented writers Brandchaft, Stolorow, and Atwood (1992) described the example of a 23-year-old man (Case I-B) who was having trouble concentrating at school. His father was assuming financial responsibility for his son's schooling and his therapy. Father resented the financial burden, and thought of his son as weak and as a source of shame for himself. At home, the patient had to wait for his father to finish a variety of activities before he could speak to the father, and then only talk about subjects the father was interested in. His mother told him when, what, and how to eat, whether he should sit or stand, and what music he liked. Whenever he attempted to assert himself, he was told that he was selfish, inconsiderate, and that his father would not come home at all if he continued to behave that way.

In the latter example, the question might arise whether or not these parents wanted their son to "grow up." Instead, did they need to have him around in order to control and criticize him? Patients with BPD are often accused of *splitting*, which is defined as an inability to integrate good and bad images of other people. It is not surprising to me, however, that this patient would have trouble putting his parents' good and bad behavior together. It was bizarre and contradictory. In fact, most therapists are hard pressed to explain this sort of behavior, and often themselves have a tendency to think in terms of the polarities of all good or all bad. Perhaps our patients who seem to "split" are thinking the way almost anyone might given a need to comprehend such an utterly confusing picture.

When I first described my own model for the genesis of BPD behavior patterns (1988), I focused on my observation that the parents of offspring with the disorder seemed to be overinvolved and often overprotective of their progeny to an exceptional and overblown degree. This overinvolvement by the parents was oddly mixed with a large degree of hostility. This pattern started when the children were born and continued into their adulthood. The combination of simultaneous overinvolvement and hostility led to the hypothesis that the parents of those with the condition are highly ambivalent about their role as parents. They seem to feel that being a parent is their full-time mission in life, yet they also feel it to be burdensome and an impediment to their own satisfaction.

My initial focus on parental overinvolvement did not incorporate the underinvolvement/neglect polarity, and therefore turned out to be only part of the picture. In order to better understand the family and individual dynamics present in the families of BPD patients, let us return to the limited empirical data about the families of patients with BPD. Unfortunately, as mentioned, there are few published empirical studies of the families of adult borderlines in the present. In the following discussions, the term *child* refers to the biological relationship of the patients to their family of origin, not to their chronological age. Later I return to the example of Case I-A and her mother and translate their argument into more understandable terms.

To reiterate, studies of the families support several seemingly dissimilar themes: neglect, abuse, parental overinvolvement, parental overprotection, and biparental failure. These themes can be conceptualized as representing a combination of or oscillation between both parental overinvolvement and underinvolvement. Overprotection, the theme that seems to show up the least, may be one subset of parental overinvolvement. The two cases that I just described are consistent with the overinvolvement dynamic, as are many case reports from a variety of sources. Some forms of abuse, such as incest, can be thought of as yet a different form of overinvolvement, to say the least. Biparental failure could also very easily lead to neglect in a variety of ways.

On first glance at many case studies, parents may seem to be either overinvolved or underinvolved, and there seems to be little or no oscillation between the two. However, I have found, along with other observers (Everett, Halperin, Volgy, & Wissler, 1989), that although the overinvolvement or underinvolvement dynamic may predominate in any given family, if one waits long enough, one eventually will see the opposite polarity. It is helpful to think of these, not as two separate patterns, but merely two sides of the same coin. The behavior of the parents of BPD is polarized at one or the other extreme, but then switches to the opposite extreme. Involvement may be over or under, but it hardly ever seems to be just right. Much as it seems to be missing in the cognitive life of the BPD patient, middle ground is a nonconcept in these families.

Several examples come to mind. One 40-year-old woman (Case I-C) told me initially that she had had no contact with her mother in several years. Later she admitted, however, that she had neglected to tell me about the 3 a.m. phone calls she had monthly with that very same mother. The calls would be characterized by an extensive verbal harangue by the mother in which the patient was harshly and roundly criticized for being a lesbian, followed by a declaration of how much the mother loved the patient. The profession of love infuriated the patient even more than the criticism. This was because the mother had beaten the patient as a child with an iron cord so many times that the patient had to be placed in a group home. Atypically, her home as a child was so aversive that she actually preferred the group home to her family home, and would purposely break the rules of the home so that she would be "punished" by being forced to stay *longer*. How could the physical abuse doled out by the mother possibly be consistent with the love of which the mother spoke?

Another patient (Case I-D) was completely ignored when she was doing well, but whenever she started to have financial problems, the mother took a tremendous interest in her plight. However, the mother refused to give the patient money, but would instead give it to the patient's 10-year-old son.

A third patient (Case I-E), a man in his mid forties, was the subject of frequent verbal harangues from his mother. She complained that he would not move in with her to take care of her. She then seemed to contradict her professed desire for this help by adding that he was so useless, he would not be of much use to her anyway. On one occasion, she punctuated that last remark by spitting in his face.

Last, a potential example was that of a single mother (Case I-F) who worked to exhaustion in two jobs so that she could afford to buy her 9-year-old daughter all of the latest designer clothes. When the girl said, "Why don't you work less so I won't have to spend so much time by myself," the mother replied, "But then I wouldn't have money to buy you all of these nice things."

The last case illustrates another rather counterintuitive idea about these families: Even when the patient with BPD is being neglected to the extreme, the parents often continue to be completely focused on the child. In cases of neglect, the parents often blame the child for being such a bad individual that of course the parents can not stand to be around him or her. If a child complains appropriately about something lacking in their lives, they are told that their selfishness is driving the parents away. Sometimes the parents seem to go out of their way to be neglectful by organizing their activities around the best way to be away from the children. All the while, the parents covertly convey to the children that the parents are obsessed with them all the time they are separated.

Even adults with the disorder who may appear to be completely estranged from their family of origin usually continue to have some contact. The hostile yet child-focused attitude of the parents is conveyed to the patient through such contacts. Consistent with Benjamin's (1993) observation, the problems of other family members continue to be blamed on the patient in some way. Lines of communication in such cases may take the form of infrequent telephone conversations or visits, during which blaming comments are made ("Your belonging to that other church is keeping me and your father awake all night"). Alternatively, messages between adult patients and their parents may be communicated through third parties, such as an aunt, a sibling, a family friend, or even a patient's ex-spouse. Occasionally, the family establishes elaborate communication networks. In families in which the parents are divorced, enmeshment with one parent may predominate, yet the other parent may often be kept informed.

Benjamin also pointed out the ongoing chaotic nature of the families of patients with BPD and how they are overtly or subtly blamed for it or somehow expected to exert control over it. I have found that at the same time that patients are expected to fix everything, they are accused of incompetence. The case of the man whose mother spit in his face is a good example of this phenomenon. This strange mix of polarized, opposite expectancies by the family—in this case both competence and incompetence—may be the origin of the *apparent competence* phenomenon described by Linehan (1993). The patient responded by subtly attempting to take charge of his mother while making it look as if she were taking care of him by depending on her financially. We come back to discuss the nature of *apparent incompetence* more extensively later on.

Linehan (1993) described yet another essential feature of the families of BPD patients. The perceptions and opinions of children are continuously invalidated. This does not merely mean that the parent disagrees with the child. An invalidation (or *disqualification*, as it is known in family systems theory) involves the implication that the child's views have no basis in reality or are utterly worthless. Invalidation can even be applied to the patient's private experiences. For example, one father said to his daughter, when she had never indicated her preferences, "Why are you eating an orange? You don't like oranges." If a child dares to question the parents about some apparent contradiction in the parents' behavior, they often deny that the behavior in question ever happened or accuse the child of "reading too much into everything." One mother of a patient would deny having said something immediately after having said it. When the daughter protested, she was accused of "living in the past."

The totality of these patterns raise two related and very important questions. First, how do individuals react when persistently subjected to this sort of treatment? Second, why do the parents act so bizarrely? In order to answer these fundamental, clinically relevant questions, I must first make detours to relevant aspects of the subjects of evolutionary biology, cognitive theory, and familial transmission of dysfunctional behavior patterns.

2

Kin Selection, Self-Sacrifice, and Family Homeostasis

In the theoretical paradigm described in this book, human beings are conceived as biological entities, whose range of responses is limited by the genetically produced structure of the human brain. However, one important facet of this phenomenon that is often neglected by those who investigate the biology of psychiatric disorders is this: One of the things that the human brain is most strongly programmed to do genetically is to be exquisitely sensitive to the social environment (Brothers, 1997; Siegal, 1999). The brain is "plastic"; that is, new neural dendritic connections are continually formed throughout the life cycle, and old ones strengthened or weakened. Much of the input that determines which connections are made, lost, strengthened, or weakened directly involves the social environment. The family environment is particularly powerful in shaping individual behavior, while the cultural environment is particularly powerful in shaping family behavior. I believe the roots of this social primacy lie in evolution and natural selection.

Belonging to a group has obvious survival value. Group survival is more likely than individual survival to ensure that the species will continue to propagate; thus, groups composed of altruistic individuals are selected for during evolution. For example, if an animal in a herd is injured and, because of the injury, slows down the movement

---

*Portions of this chapter previously appeared in Allen & Farmer, 1996, and Allen, 2001.

of the entire group, the group becomes a much easier target for predators. If, on the other hand, the injured animal separates itself from the herd, and the rest of the herd leaves it to die, the herd is freer to move on to safer ground. Therefore, the likelihood increases that more animals will survive long enough to reproduce. An adaptive genetic mutation does little good for its own survival or the survival of the species if the animal with the mutation is killed off prior to reproducing itself. Genes that lead to a tendency of animals to sacrifice themselves for the good of the group, as well as those genes that lead to a tendency to sacrifice the other members of the herd when necessary, will tend to be selected for and passed on to future generations.

In biology, this idea is known as kin or group selection (Wilson, 1998). This idea posits that individuals within coherent social groups are altruistic in many contexts. We inherit an inborn tendency to be willing to sacrifice our own needs whenever such needs are in conflict with the needs of the kin group. In some circumstances, parents will even sacrifice their own children if the group deems it necessary.

The tendency of people to sacrifice themselves for the group to which they belong can be readily inferred from the willingness of most individuals to die for their family or their country when these groups are under threat. The idea that one should not necessarily be willing to go to war and die if the group demanded it was not seriously questioned by a significant proportion of the population until the Vietnam war spiraled out of control in the mid 1960s. As I described in previous work (1988, 1991), the balance of collectivist tendencies and individualist philosophies has slowly been shifting, as culture as evolved, toward the latter.

The sacrifice of children can be readily observed in such phenomena as female infanticide in China and honor killings in the Middle East. In the United States during World War II, mothers who lost children in battle were dubbed "Gold Star" mothers. They were highly honored and given special recognition. Again, this idea of child sacrifice was not seriously challenged until the 1960s. I recall when an antiwar rock group called Country Joe and the Fish facetiously exhorted mothers to "Be the first one on your block to have your boy come home in a box." The appeal of the Jesus story, in which God sacrifices His only son for the good of humanity, possibly may be due to its connection with this biological tendency.

The concept of group selection remains controversial among evolutionary biologists and is, in fact, only accepted by a minority of them. The reasons for this lack of acceptance often appear to be more aesthetic or political than scientific. One biologist once told me that he did not accept it because it would "lead to fascism." His fear was that it could be used as justification for the elimination of the weaker elements in society for the good of the group. I believe that this biological process did, in fact, lead to fascism in the 20th century. In a sense, it is why we had fascist regimes. Fortunately, the group behaviors that characterize civilization also evolve along with individuals, and group structure has changed so that such ideas and behavior are no longer deemed desirable.

The idea that human beings are genetically predisposed, although not predetermined, to sacrifice their own idiosyncratic needs for the perceived good of the rest of the family is often difficult for Americans to understand because their ambient culture seems to value self-actualization and individualism (Allen, 1991). This sets up an interesting paradox: The ambient culture is the group, and the group demands individuality. The group says to us, "We will make you independent." Of course, if individuals are merely bowing to group pressure, they are not in fact acting independently. The paradox is at the heart of a ubiquitous human dialectical struggle posited by Kerr and Bowen (1988) between the forces of togetherness and the forces of individuality.

An understanding of the hidden altruism in human behavior leads to a new twist in theories about the so-called repetition compulsion. For example, Gold and Wachtel (1993) in their theory of cyclical psychodynamics address the issue of why individuals persist in the same interpersonal patterns over and over again with the same predictable, unpleasant consequences. They opine that the aims of an action are not equivalent to the consequences of that action and add, "The consequence [of their actions] is predictable, of course, not from the vantage point of the individuals who blindly repeat the problematic pattern over and over, but from the vantage point of the observer not trapped in the pattern" (p. 375).

A difficulty with this formulation involves the question of why something that is predictable to everyone else does not seem to be predictable from the person thusly "trapped." Gold and Wachtel (1993) hypothesized that this "neurotic stupidity" (p. 61) stems from blind spots created by anxiety over certain ideas. The idea that anxiety leads to repression of cognitive information has a long and storied history in psychotherapy, and seems quite reasonable on the surface. However, I do not believe that anxiety prevents one from eventually noticing blatantly obvious, recurrent consequences to one's stereo-typed actions, even when the consequences are highly anxiety-provoking and therefore very unpleasant. If anything, the unpleasant nature of the consequences should make them rather salient.

Applying the idea of hidden altruism obviates the need to posit stupidity or the avoidance of anxiety about information that pro-duces cognitive dissonance as the primary explanation for the repe-tition compulsion. I believe that anxiety avoidance does come into play in a different way: Individuals have an inborn tendency to wish to avoid the existential terror that comes into play when they defy their kin group (Allen, 1988). This phenomenon is discussed in greater detail later.

In order to understand the process by which hidden altruism man-ifests itself in repetitive behavior, let us examine an often-used sche-matic example of a negative, repeating interpersonal interaction—the case of the alcoholic husband and the nagging wife. The nagger says she nags because the drinker drinks, and vice versa. In fact, they say this to each other all the time. Nonetheless, they persist in nagging and drinking, when this behavior does not lead to change. Why?

Each may be discounting the role of his or her own contribution to the problem for any number of reasons. In my opinion, however, the wife *has to know* that, at the very least, the husband is using her nagging as a pretext to drink. He may drink anyway, but nagging certainly does not solve the problem. It exacerbates it. The husband tells her so, and the results bear this out. Similarly, the husband has to know that his continued drinking leads to more nagging. As a further complication, both know that the *other* member of the cou-ple persists in the behavior knowing full well what the conse-quences will be. The other member will neither change nor leave the relationship. How does each explain to himself or herself the behavior of the other?

Indeed, one could argue that the nagger nags *in order* to give the drinker an excuse to drink, and the drinker drinks in order to give the nagger an excuse to nag. I suggest that each member of the cou-ple is engaging in the behavior, at great personal sacrifice, because he or she believes that it is the *other* person who needs and wants the relationship to continue in its current dysfunctional form. The compulsive, persistent, and repetitive nature of the behavior, combined with the mutual knowledge of the obvious consequences for the relationship, reinforces this idea in each member of the couple.

If this formulation is correct, neither member of the couple would admit to having such beliefs to anyone, least of all each other. There are two reasons for this. First, the member of the couple hearing such an opinion would very likely attack the speaker for misplaced blame. How dare a husband blame his own misbehavior on his wife! At best, the speaker who initiated the conversation would be accused of rationalizing his or her own sick behavior. Second, third parties—including therapists—would tell the speaker how ridiculous such an idea is. Why on earth would anyone want to continue in such a terrible relationship?

Many couples in therapy routinely express the baffling idea that if the relationship changes in the direction championed by the therapist—and seemingly requested by the couple themselves—it will end. I propose that each thinks it will end because, they believe, in spite of the spouse's verbal protestations to the contrary, that the other member of the couple really wants it to continue in its current form.

I have found that when I pose a question about this kind of belief in just the right way and at just the right time, the members of the couple usually will admit to having such thoughts about their respective spouses. Additionally, they often have come up with an explanation for the seemingly masochistic "needs" of the other person in the relationship. These explanations are often pseudo-psychoanalytic formulations. Psychoanalytic ideas have become ingrained in the common culture and have become part of the lexicon. For example, the wife in our schematic example may believe that the husband "needs" her to keep nagging so that he will continue to be able to displace onto her his otherwise unacceptable (to him) anger at his own nagging mother. Interestingly, I find that spouses are often experts on their in-laws. When I ask about family history, the spouse may supply information that the patient does not even know.

Both members of any intimate relationship, by persisting in behavior in the face of obvious negative consequences, seem to be "asking for it." People use that phrase facetiously, but I am suggesting that they really do believe it. My patient who struck her mother in a therapy session (Case I-A) could easily interpret her mother's behavior—berating her and pushing her face toward the patient as she was becoming angry—as a *request* to be hit. But why would anyone want to stay in a bad relationship pattern? Why would anyone want to be abused? Are they in fact masochists?

I do not believe that individuals stuck in repetitive negative interactions really do "want" the bad parts of the relationship. Rather that they are somehow more comfortable with them than without them. This distinction is not a matter of splitting hairs; mixed feelings are a hallmark of psychodynamic conflict. The concept of an intrapsychic *conflict* over role function is as useful in understanding interpersonal behavior as it is in understanding individual psychopathology. Spouses are being truthful when they object so vehemently when confronted about their behavior; of course they do not enjoy the nagging or drinking that they seem to incessantly provoke. However, that is only half of the picture. If the full truth were told, they are ambivalent about it. They experience both a need for the negative interactions *and* a wish that they would stop.

Before discussing further how such a strange state of affairs comes to be, I must first address the question of responsibility of the adult victim in an abusive relationship. Lest I be accused of "blaming the victim," I will state clearly that I strongly believe that there is no justification for beating or otherwise grossly mistreating anyone. No one is entitled to strike another person, no matter if they had been provoked, and no matter how severe any provocation may have been. This is not to say, however, than an adult in a western country who is the victim of abuse bears no responsibility whatsoever for what has occurred.

As Michael Kerr (personal communication) has pointed out, both "It's *all* my fault" and "I had *nothing* to do with it" are highly unrealistic positions to take in understanding the issue of responsibility in interpersonal relationships. A woman in most westernized cultures may feel as if she were a psychological prisoner of an abusive spouse because of the process I am describing, but from a practical standpoint, she now has many options for successfully leaving the relationship. Certainly men may threaten bodily harm and sometimes even kill if a lover leaves, but over the long term, the cumulative risk of severe harm is actually much higher as a function of the length of time a woman remains in an abusive situation. If a woman stays in an abusive relationship, and especially if she continually proclaims her "love" for the abuser as is so often the case, the abuser will interpret this behavior to mean that she loves him *the way he is.*

Of course, in more traditional, collectivist cultures, options for women to get out of a bad relationship may not exist. In cases where there are no realistic options, the victim bears little responsibility for what happens to her. This is decidedly not the case in the industrialized west.

I believe that when two individuals are stuck in repetitive dysfunction interactions, what makes these patterns more comfortable than their absence is that the relationship as it stands allows each to continue to play a role within his or her own family of origin—again, at great personal sacrifice. Because of their genetic programming, they will sacrifice their own happiness if the family of origin seems to require it, and each member of the couple helps the other to continue to do so. There is indeed some truth in the pseudo-psychoanalytic explanation that the spouses envision.

Unified Therapy (Allen 1988, 1991, 1993), the therapy paradigm on which this book is based, posits a tendency of members of a couple who share unacknowledged ambivalence to reinforce for one another role behavior learned in their respective families of origin. They each believe that that is exactly what is expected of them. This is called "dialectic cross-motive reading" and is similar in some respects to the Alcoholics Anonymous concept of "enabling." As Gold and Wachtel (1993) stated (p. 61), "every neurosis requires accomplices." The Unified Therapy perspective is compatible with Benjamin's (1993) observation that every pathology is a gift of love. When I inquire about what family members are saying about a couple's problems, I often find that the respective families of origin seem to act in ways that reinforce the couple's negative behavior toward each other.

This view is similar to a family systems assumption that may seem absurd to someone who views patients in isolation from their social system. In their famous book *Paradox and Counterparadox,* Palazzoli and associates (1978) described how individuals sacrifice their own needs for the perceived needs of their family of origin as described previously. Family systems therapists look at the process from the perspective of the group rather than the individual. They use the term *family homeostasis* to describe how self-sacrificing behavior plays out within the group.

Families, like any group of people with a purpose, must have a set of rules by which various tasks are assigned to individual members. Without such rules, chaos would prevail because no one in the family would know who, if anyone, was responsible for fulfilling various important group functions. In order for the group to function smoothly, each member of the family should know what roles and obligations are expected of him or her. Once the rules are established, they are often no longer discussed. Unless the rules can be discussed in a meaningful way, any individual in the family who steps out of line is pushed back toward his or her usual role by the rest of the family in a manner to be described shortly. This later phenomenon is called family homeostasis because the group enforces individual behavior so that it stays within a certain range, not unlike the way the body keeps the blood electrolyte levels within a certain range—a process known in biology as physiological homeostasis. If an individual would rather behave in ways clearly outside of the prescribed range, he or she will then sacrifice this desire.

If individuals are thusly controlled by the apparent needs of their family of origin, how then can we explain the high incidence of oppositional behavior in dysfunctional families? The answer is that, if an individual seems to be oppositional, it is only because the individual perceives the family as *needing* him or her to be oppositional. Paradoxically, the only way the family seems to be placated is when the oppositional individual is defying its verbal instructions. I described in detail how such an odd state of affairs comes about in a previous work (Allen, 1991).

In general, how does the process by which an individual is induced to sacrifice his or her own needs for the good of the family work? In particular, how do the behavior patterns of patients with BPD come about? In what way do they stabilize the patient's family of origin? In order to answer these questions, we first need to look at the process from a cognitive perspective.

COGNITIVE SCHEMATA IN BPD

Human beings are, of course, thinking creatures. With an inborn tendency toward evaluating and meeting group needs, we might hypothesize that children would attempt to read their parents' behavior in order to find out what the family needs. They could then try out different behavior to see what is or is not going to be accept-able. After the trial-and-error learning process is complete, the acceptable behavior then becomes automatic and "unconscious" in familiar appearing situations. The reason for this again has to do with normal brain functioning. If we had to consciously deliberate about every simple thing we do, we would be paralyzed. Hence, the brain is genetically set to subconsciously attend to familiar environmental cues, which then activate previously learned but now automatic response patterns.

When faced with unfamiliar social situations, individuals attempt to influence others to behave in ways consistent with the social behavior in their own families. If successful in doing so, they have no need to alter mental models of how interpersonal exchanges are supposed to be negotiated. If consistently unsuccessful, however, they may be forced to rethink those patterns that had previously been learned on a trial-and-error basis.

When children get a confusing double message, and seem to be in the wrong no matter how they behave, the task of ascertaining the needs of the family system becomes infinitely more difficult. In today's western, "postmodern" society, confusion over roles and relationships is rampant in people of all ages. As we discuss later, the conflictual behavior patterns of parents of patients with BPD falls into the category of role ambivalence and confusion.

The concept of *schemata* or mental models is useful in understanding the learning process of children attempting to find out what behavior is acceptable, as well as the interpersonal response patterns of the BPD patient within the family. Horowitz (1988) defined "role relationship schemata" as working mental models of various types of important social relationships. These models serve as guidelines for interpersonal behavior and allow one to predict the intentions of others. Such models often contain extensive "scripts" (Steiner, 1971) that involve prototypical sequences of interaction in various social contexts. Scripts may define lifetime patterns of behavior. Role-relationship schemata are felt by Horowitz to originate in childhood, but new versions can be built throughout life through the processes of accommodation to and assimilation of new environmental demands (Ivey, 1986). In familiar-appearing social situations, however, old schemata are activated. Such schemata may be continually activated and strengthened most potently by parental behavior throughout the life span.

How do such schemata develop when children receive conflicting, contradictory, or highly ambiguous information when attempting to discern how they are supposed to act in certain family and social situations? Most role-relationship schemata initially form during a period when the individual has not yet arrived at the Piagetian stage of cognitive development (Ginsburg & Opper, 1969) known as "formal operations." Children who have not yet reached this stage of development would be very unlikely to come up with the explanation that their parents themselves are confused and conflicted about the matter at hand.

Research by social psychologists using three completely different methodologies (Donaldson & Westerman, 1986; Harter, 1986; Selman, 1980) indicates that the concept of ambivalence in human motivation does not begin to develop until the ages of 10 to 15 years old. Practical application of such knowledge often does not come into play until considerably later than that. Unfortunately, cognitive schemata about role functioning in interpersonal relationships tend to develop far earlier in life, and tend to become almost reflexive or automatic in familiar-appearing situations. Children and adults will tend to react to significant others as though they had only a single goal or desire in each type of situation. This by no means indicates that adults function at the cognitive level of children, only that one often does not stop to think about habitual behavior if it seems to work.

As an aside, Westen (1991) pointed out that the research on cognition described earlier is inconsistent with the psychoanalytic view that normal human children learn to integrate good and bad images of their parents during the "rapprochement" phase of separation–individuation. That period occurs around 2 years of age. Patients with BPD are thought by some analysts to have had a developmental arrest at that age, and are therefore deficient in their integrative capabilities. This is posited as the reason that they seem to engage in "splitting" as a defense. If, in fact, normal children do not understand the concept of mixed motivation until much later in life, it seems unlikely that they would be able to successfully learn to integrate good and bad images at that early age. Interestingly, patients with BPD are also considered by some to be master manipulators, a talent that would seem to require that an individual be able to assess someone else's strong and weak points simultaneously. Although it is quite true that patients with the disorder on occasion act *as if* they lack this ability, I believe that the deficit is more apparent than real.

When individuals grow up, their parents usually continue to act in ways that recapitulate social interactional sequences from the patient's early life experience. This parental behavior automatically both cues and reinforces old but engrained role-relationship schemata. In turn, these reinforced schemata become more likely to be activated in the patient's current social interactions. This leads to reenactment and recapitulation of these patterns in other relationships. As mentioned, if the behavior patterns lead to novel responses from important outsiders in the environment, the individual will attempt to induce these others to conform to their needs and expectations, or may instead quickly break off such relationships.

Parental behavior seems to be an extremely potent environmental reinforcer for previously learned social behavior. This most likely stems from the survival value of coherent group structure in evolution. As psychoanalysts have hypothesized, children internalize the values and role behaviors of their social system, and conformity to the group has in the past continued to have survival value throughout the life cycle. Parental behavior has such a powerful effect in triggering old schemata that it does not have to occur with any great degree of frequency in order for its effects to continue. In adults, the reinforcement of schemata occurs in a manner analogous to the learning theory paradigm of a variable intermittent reinforcement schedule. That is, the powerful parental behavior may be witnessed infrequently but unpredictably, leading the patient to continue to react rigidly in ways consistent with old role-relationship expectations.

Family-systems therapists have noted that when patients attempt to make changes from previous role-function behavior, they are often actively if not violently discouraged by other family members. In this situation, family members disqualify or disconfirm one another, consensually invalidating new behavior. Disqualification can also be conceived in self-psychological terms as a refusal to consensually *mirror* such behavior. *Mirroring* is a process of validation of an individual's sense of self by parental figures (Kohut, 1971, 1977). Family invalidation of new behavior may make change exceedingly difficult and also reinforces the individual's tendency to engage in previously learned, self-sacrificing role-relationship patterns.

During script formation, response patterns are probably dictated by an individual's perception of the needs of the parents rather than directly by the parental behavior itself (Allen, 1991). That is, when individuals respond to unfamiliar parental behavior, they attempt to determine what the parents expect from them within that context. The idea that children assess the needs and inclinations of significant others and that such behavior may be part of the human bonding process was advanced by Bowlby (1988).

THE SPOILER ROLE IN BPD

In the case of patients with BPD, apparently oppositional and self-destructive behavior is triggered by their perceptions of the needs of the parents. I have described in detail how people generally read one another's motives in confusing situations in a previous work (1991). In the case of the borderline family, the affected individual looks at the parents' incomprehensible actions, and has trouble balancing their seeming preoccupation with him or her with their seeming anger and wish for avoidance. We need not posit any genetic cognitive deficits to see that this would be a difficult task for anyone. Children in these families see at a very young age that the parents' lives seem to revolve around them. If the child were to become truly independent—again, at no matter what age—the parents seem to fall apart.

For example, one patient (Case 2-A), who lived independently but chronically found ways to subvert her own success, was asked what problems would be created for her if she were to stop doing that. Specifically, who around her might be negatively affected? The patient replied instantly that her parents would get angry and would not know what to do with themselves. Furthermore, they would stop sending her money. Another patient (Case 2-B) was disinherited in favor of his loafing, freeloading, troublemaking brother. When he asked his parents why they wrote the will that way, they replied, "But you're doing so well, you're successful. You don't need the money; your brother does!"

How does the child read the anger of the parent in the context of child-focused yet hostile parents? I suggest that the child forms not one conclusion, but two: First, despite parental verbal protestations, absences, and other seeming contradictions, the parents must need the child to be around. Second, the reason they need the child around is to have someone on whom they can take out their frustrations, and on whom they can blame the family's misfortunes.

Once a child forms these ideas, how then does he or she give these parents what they seem to need? As it turns out, one excellent and often used solution to this problem is to engage in behavior that has been given the label of *spoiling*. Spoiling is the prototypical hostile, demanding, self-destructive, and provocative behavior so frequently described in the clinical literature on BPD. The term was used initially by Kleinian psychoanalysts to describe behavior they thought to be a reflection of primitive anger, based on envy, at the nourishing mother's breast (Kernberg, 1994).

This behavior, in my opinion, more likely stems from the ongoing, as well as present-day, contingencies in the families of BPD patients that I described earlier (Allen & Farmer, 1996). In essence, the child continuously makes direct or indirect demands on the parents, even if physically separated from them, while ruining or destroying all of the parents' efforts to "take care" of the patient. In this way, the child enables the parents to continue to focus their lives around the child while blaming him or her for all of their ills. Spoiling behavior also provides the parents with a justification for both past and ongoing abusive behavior.

The "spoiler" fails at a variety of endeavors and becomes involved in dangerous activities, while spitefully blaming the parents for all of these problems. In response, parents may frequently bail their adult children out of trouble and then withdraw in disgust. For example, many such patients have been through multiple, costly therapies and drug rehabilitation centers at their parents' expense—without appreciable improvement. They may even leave programs against advice, and then ask the parents to pay for more treatment later on.

Individuals engaging in spoiling behavior often report a belief, based on past experience, that, if they stop acting in this contradictory manner, the parents will become increasingly more depressed, angry, combative, or self-destructive. For example, a father's alcohol problem may be exacerbated. Furthermore, when these patients do well in life, they are often ignored, criticized, or otherwise disqualified in the manner described by Benjamin (1993).

The spoiler role is a difficult one, and the patient will often find spouses or lovers whose behavior helps him or her stay "in character." The patient with BPD often needs the accomplices that were mentioned earlier. For example, a woman who has BPD may choose an abusive husband who loses his job, gambles away savings, and interferes with her career advancement. This puts her in a situation where she has a convenient reason to go to her parents for financial aid. The parents may try to mediate the spousal disputes, but the couple's behavior makes the parents' failure in this endeavor inevitable. The parents then withdraw in anger. The husband's behavior thusly assists the patient in creating a situation in which her parents can maintain alternating overinvolvement with and withdrawal from the patient. Additionally, the husband's behavior partially deflects the parents' rage on to him, thereby sparing the patient some unpleasant experiences with her parents. Ultimately, the parents' anger falls back on their daughter because she refuses to leave her husband.

Most men would be unwilling to act in such a manner; if it became apparent that a woman in a new relationship was acting in a spoiling fashion, they would be quickly frightened away. However, if a man has similar issues in his own family, such that having a demanding yet help-rejecting wife helps him to play a required role in his family of origin, he might very well be attracted to a woman with BPD. The needs of each member of a couple to have accomplices in order to play an egodystonic role are often reciprocal. The "help" each one receives from the other in playing their respective roles is referred to in family systems theory as the *marital quid pro quo*. Women with BPD, for example, often marry men with narcissistic personality disorder. The narcissistic role can be complementary to the spoiler role, as we shall see later in the chapter when we look at the "little man."

The concept of spoiling, combined with the pattern of hostile parental overinvolvement and underinvolvement, can account for several of the DSM IV (APA, 1994) diagnostic criteria for BPD. The parents' alternating, polarized, angry, and confusing behavior and their contradictory role expectations of their child may help create confusion in the child about his or her place in the social system and lead to an unstable identity. Parental preoccupation with the patient's dysfunctional or sick behavior to the exclusion of his or her healthy or autonomous behavior may trigger self-destructiveness and impulsivity. The patient's belief that the parents' functioning will decompensate should he or she not remain the center of the par-

ents' attention may contribute to the patient's panic over abandonment, as the withdrawal of parental attention may at times suggest
to the patient a prelude to the breakdown of his or her family system. Seeking abusive peers or lovers with the goal of finding someone to enable the spoiler role leads to a pattern of intense and
unstable interpersonal relationships.

The spoiling child refuses to grow up, remains dependent in some
way on the parent or a parent surrogate, and ruins everything the parents try to give. In the case of the previously described child whose
mother worked two jobs (Case I-F), the child might start to lose or
mistreat her valuable designer clothes, and then demand both re-
placement of the expensive gifts *and* more of her mother's time.

To reiterate, spoiling behavior allows fulfillment of both of the
parents' seemingly contradictory needs by allowing the borderline
patient to remain central in the parents life—even if contact seems
very limited—while providing them with an easy justification for
taking their anger out on the patient. The understanding of this dynamic becomes very important for reducing negative transference
reactions in therapy with borderlines, as is discussed in Part II.

We can view borderline behavior from another angle. James
Masterson (1981) described a pattern of behavior in patients with
BPD that he called the *borderline triad*. I would like to take a look at
this formulation through the lens of family systems theory. Simply
put, the borderline triad as posited by Masterson consists of a three-
part process:

1. When the patient with BPD attempts to individuate or function
   autonomously from his or her family, this leads to:
2. A depression that stems from a sense of abandonment, which
   then leads to:
3. Defenses such as splitting and projective identification.

Looking at this formulation from an interpersonal perspective, I
propose changing the terminology slightly and inserting an extra
step in the process. First, I suggest substituting Bowen's (1978)
term *differentiation of self* for the more psychoanalytic term *separation and individuation*. These terms are often used interchangeably
by clinicians, but there is a difference. In my view, separation–individuation is something that happens to all neurologically intact

people in our culture. I believe there is in fact no such thing as a true developmental arrest except in unimaginably severe cases of environmental trauma, such as those in which basic nutritional needs are not met. One can no more be stopped from individuating than from growing.

However, one may be afraid of *expressing* one's unique needs and perspectives, and may pretend to be something one is not. Differentiation of self refers to this latter process; it is something one does as opposed to something one is. The BPD patient's dysfunctional behavior represents, in reference to the third part of the borderline triad, a defensive false self. At some point in the patient's life when he or she reaches a certain inevitable level of cognitive development, it becomes a conscious although seldom thought-about choice the patient with BPD makes.

What happens when a borderline patient attempts to differentiate from his or her family of origin? As described earlier, he or she becomes subjected to family disqualification or invalidation. This is the additional step I propose to add to the borderline triad. The disqualification by the family in such an instance takes the form of one of a large variety of ways in which a person is told, in effect, "You are wrong, change back." Consensual validation is withheld. The case I mentioned earlier of the man (Case 1-B) who was told that he was being selfish and driving his father away from home is a good example. Another example came from the case history of a woman (Case 2-C) who was screamed at by her mother when the patient attempted to get out of a 20-year loveless relationship with her husband. The mother blasted the patient, saying, "I cannot believe you are doing this! I'm going to write your husband and apologize for your behavior. And don't you know that you're going to *destroy your children!*" Benjamin (1993) mentioned the reaction of some of the parents of her borderlines to the success of the patient: "You think you're great because of *that!* Let me set the record straight. You're just an [expletive] kid, and when you get out into the world and try to make it without us, you'll find out what a [expletive] kid you are" (p. 120).

When individuals are disqualified or invalidated by their family of origin, they experience a terrifying mix of anxiety and depression that goes by many different names and takes many different forms, but is one of the most awful feelings we ever experience (Allen,

1988). It is called *anomie* in sociology, and it is also called existential groundlessness, derealization, depersonalization, and fragmentation. It entails a sense of not being real, valid, or valued. It is experienced as an absence of the normal orienting cues in the world that tell us how to behave in our social world. Patients will speak of a sense of going crazy or a feeling of feeling annihilated. There is a sense that, "If I am not as I was, then I do not exist."

In response to disqualification, the borderline gives up autonomy and self assertion, and falls right back into a false self. In particular, the false self of the patient with BPD is one that exhibits the various and sundry manifestations of spoiling behavior.

As mentioned earlier, the strange mix of polarized, opposite expectancies by the family of the patient with BPD—in this case both competence and incompetence—may be the origin of the *apparent competence* phenomenon described by Linehan (1993). She pointed out that borderlines use passivity as a strategy in some interpersonal contexts with little real success, while in other contexts demonstrate surprising "apparent" competence. Such shifts may take place even in situations in which the patient is not overtly experiencing emotional upheaval. She wisely avoided the nonsensical claim that individuals can demonstrate, by performance, competencies that they do not in fact possess. Instead, she opines that sometimes patients with BPD have an inability to generalize their skills to certain situations. At other times, however, she states that they have a tendency to overgeneralize.

A dialectic synthesis of these polarities requires that both parts of the contradiction be incorporated into the same formulation. One such hypothesis is that patients with BPD hide their competency in some situations because certain environmental demands require this. Acting this way might paradoxically be the most competent thing they could do—somewhat like an educated Cambodian pretending to be an illiterate peasant in order to prevent persecution by the Khmer Rouge in the 1970s. In terms of our present discussion, patients with BPD may act in an incompetent manner in order to competently reduce the overall level of their parents' distress. Their only "incompetence" is their understandable difficulty in making sense of their parents' peculiar proclivities.

Despite many common themes in the behavior of patients with BPD and their families, patients with BPD are clearly an extremely heterogeneous group. In the next section, we discuss the reasons for the wide variation in the clinical presentations of these patients.

VARIATIONS OF BPD AND COMORBID PERSONALITY DISORDERS

Borderline personality disorder, like all personality disorders, is not a disease in any real sense; it is merely a combination of dysfunctional traits that tend to occur together more often than one would predict by chance. In order to meet DSM criteria for BPD, one must exhibit at least five of nine possible criteria—*any* five. Of course, one could also have any six, seven, or eight characteristics of the disorder, or perhaps all nine. If we were to rate each criterion on a five-point severity scale, it is easy to see that there are literally hundreds of different ways to have the disorder.

Additionally, once an individual reaches the threshold of any DSM-III or IV personality disorder, it is quite likely that they will exhibit other comorbid personality disorders. These additional disorders can be any of those listed in the DSM, including any from clusters A, B, or C. Patients with BPD may also suffer from multiple Axis I disorders, including affective, anxiety, dissociative, somatoform, and eating disorders. Again, a given individual may have one or several of these axis I disorders, and not necessarily the same ones. Multiply the number of ways to have BPD by the number of permutations and combinations of other comorbid Axis I and II disorders, there are literally hundreds of thousands of different clinical presentations.

Although the families of patients with BPD have many common characteristics, they too are extremely heterogeneous. The parents behave differently over various issues, and also vary in the severity of dysfunctional interactional patterns. Clearly most but not all are either sexually, physically, or verbally abusive, or exhibit any combination of these types of abuse. Some families invalidate only a limited number of types of behaviors, ideas, or perceptions, whereas others attack on a much wider front. Some are more or less prone to violence. In fact, although many of the same conflictual issues exist in families that produce offspring with the disorder, there is no one single necessary or sufficient family interactional pattern required to produce it in those offspring. Furthermore, the biological temperament and reactivity of family members, including the affected individual, also varies widely. This leads to still more variants of individuals with the disorders and the families that spawn them.

Which particular combination of traits and comorbid personality disorders a given patient will exhibit is, in my opinion, determined by the interaction between genetic and temperamental predispositions and predilections of that affected individual and the different issues over which the parents create conflictual expectations. Some of the latter have been described using the concept of dysfunctional family "roles" (Allen, 1988; Slipp, 1984).

Dysfunctional roles are those behaviors on the part of offspring that seem to stabilize the parents' emotional state, and therefore family homeostasis, in some way. They usually occur in contexts in which the parents have a specific conflict over some role that they feel they must play because of their experiences in their own family of origin, but which they may actively dislike playing. In the next chapter, I discuss how and why some individuals develop severe conflicts over the parenting role as a whole, which I believe to be the primary conflict that produces the bizarre behavior that was described in the last chapter.

I now provide a brief overview of dysfunctional family roles. The role of the *spoiler* in the borderline family has already been described. Instead or in addition to spoiler, the individual in a dysfunctional family system may play any one or more of the roles about to be described. These roles may co-exist; depending on the current state of the family dynamics, one or another role may be manifested, alone or in combination, at any given time. These roles often blend into one another or subtly shift from time to time.

Because the parental behavior to which the patient is reacting is conflictual, all of the roles contain a devilish double bind: The parent will seem to need the role to be played, and support the patient for playing it, to an extent. However, if the patient plays the role *too* well or successfully, he or she is criticized or attacked. Patients in psychotherapy who are trapped in one of these binds will often first allude to them by making a nonspecific comment about the parents such as "Nothing I ever do pleases them."

The roles include:

1. The *Savior*: In this scenario, a parent has suppressed his or her ambition to excel at some endeavor in order to satisfy cultural mandates, leading the child to act out the forbidden ambition. The savior role often leads to chronic depression in the patient playing the role. For example, a woman from a traditional culture who has been exposed to female professionals in the United States might secretly wish to become a doctor. She can admit such a wish to neither herself nor anyone else, for fear of being disowned by her traditional relatives who expect her to be nothing more than a wife and mother.

    Because parents often live vicariously through identification with their children, the woman might push her son or possibly even a daughter to become a doctor. This child becomes the parent's "savior." Whether the mother's "stage mother" behavior initially produces a conflict in the child depends on whether or not that child had a natural inclination to become a doctor. However, even if the child were so inclined, a conflict will develop as the child gets closer to the goal. If the son or daughter succeeds in getting through medical school, the mother may, for example, become depressed.

    The reason that the mother becomes depressed is that the child's success reminds her that she herself was not able to do what she had really wanted to do all along. When she reacts negatively to the child, she is in reality covertly thinking about her own disappointments. From the perspective of the child, however, it can easily look as if the mother never really wanted him or her to become a doctor in the first place. The child becomes depressed because success becomes equated with a sense of helplessness and futility over keeping the parent stable.

2. The *Avenger*: The avenger acts out a parent's forbidden anger and hostility. This often leads the avenger to develop antisocial traits. For example, a father who is angry at his own employer but who was expected by his own Depression-era parents to keep his nose to the grindstone may react with not-so-hidden glee when his son creates havoc at the son's place of employment. If the son keeps it up, however, father then feels obligated to be critical, for two reasons. First, he was taught that such flagrant self-expression is wrong in employment contexts. Second, he really does not want to see his son lose his job.

3. The *Defective*: This role often leads to somatization or chronic psychological impairment. It is often seen in families with traditional gender role conflicts. The parents may or may not be conflicted over the role of parent per se, but feel useless when they are no longer needed in their capacity as traditional family caretakers. Children of course grow up, and the empty nest approaches. During this period, the parents have fantasies about being free from family obligations and indulging in their more individualistic tendencies. Unfortunately, they feel useless and vaguely guilty if they indulge them.

   The child of such parents fears becoming independent for fear the parents might develop a pathological empty nest syndrome. He or she responds by failing to become self-sufficient. So that the parents do not blame themselves for the child's lack of independence, or feel as though they had been inadequate parents, the child blames this inability to take care of himself or herself on some physical or psychological disorder. The actual disorder may or may not be present, and if present, may or may not be exaggerated. Often it is unclear whether or not the child is *purposely* exaggerating his or her apparent disability. This way, depending on whether the parent is feeling guilty or angry at a given time, the child can assuage one polarity and feed into the other. He or she attempts to regulate exactly how much of each their parents' are experiencing, in order to provide maximum stability.

4. The *Go Between*: In this situation, the child is triangulated into a conflictual parental marriage. One or both parents may use the child as a confidant to complain about the other parent. Sometimes the parent may even have the child act as a sort of surrogate spouse, and act the way he or she really wishes the spouse would act. In the latter scenario, if the parent–child relationship has any sexual overtones, the child may exhibit histrionic traits. Sometimes as adults, go-betweens are "on call" to settle marital disputes. Mother might come over and say to a grown daughter, "Go tell your father to do such and such; he won't do it if I ask him but he will for you." If the daughter complies, the mother may become jealous of her child's relationship with the father.

5. *Little Man*: This scenario is a variant of the savior role that leads to narcissistic issues. It is usually seen in males but may occur

in a slightly different form with females. Gender-role conflicts once again are the main culprit. In this situation, a woman who may have been taught as a child to be dependent on men and defer to men for most major decisions marries a man who is inadequate in some way. She may describe him as "never there for me." He may be a poor provider due to a general unwillingness to work hard or even desert the family altogether. The woman then turns to her son to take care of her in all the ways his father did not. However, the son fails in this role for two reasons. One, he may be too young and simply lack the capabilities to look after her; he probably needs his mother to take care of *him*. Second, the mother resents his attempts at looking after her and subverts them. The reason for this is that she really is not—nor does she really want to be—as dependent as she may appear to be. The more the son tries to meet her needs, the more the mother emasculates him.

A male with narcissistic personality disorder may marry a female with BPD. Such a union is a common couple type seen in marital therapy and is an excellent example of the marital quid pro quo described earlier. The female with BPD is almost a prototype of a woman who seems to need to be taken care of, but who spoils any attempt by anyone to do so. The relationship of the narcissistic male with his mother is thusly re-created in even more extreme form within the marital relationship.

To briefly summarize this chapter, the phenomenon of kin selection leads individuals to sacrifice idiosyncratic desires in order to play a role that helps maintain family homeostasis. These roles are encoded into the human brain through the development of cognitive schemata that are then automatically played out in all major social relationships, and reinforced through sporadic but continual contact with the family of origin. In the families of patients with BPD, parents are preoccupied with their children yet seem to be hostile toward them. This parental behavior evokes spoiling responses in the children. The patient with BPD may also act out other dysfunctional roles depending on other family conflicts, and may recruit accomplices in an attempt to stay in these unpleasant roles.

This formulation naturally leads back to the question of why the parents in the families of BPD patients have a dramatic love–hate relationship with their own children. Let us now return to the parents in the families of the BPD patient so that we might better understand their mysterious behavior. What on earth makes them act that way?

3

Parental Role Confusion

As we have seen, the parents of patients with BPD are seemingly focused on their children nearly to the point of obsession, yet simultaneously angry with them. One way to understand the parents' contradictory and seemingly irrational behavior within the families of BPD patients is to conceptualize it as a reaction to a severe and highly pervasive intrapsychic conflict over the parenting role. This conflict is created and reinforced by the parents' experience within their own families of origin. Ambivalence over being a parent is the parent's core conflictual relationship theme (Luborsky & Crits-Cristoph, 1990). They feel as if it is their solemn duty to sacrifice everything for their children, but at the same time they feel overwhelmed by the responsibility and resentful of the sacrifices. They may rebel against this duty, suddenly abandon their offspring and run off for an extended vacation, only to come back in guilt and shame over having done so. In the process, they feel ashamed of their confusion and therefore deny those very emotions to everyone. Alternatively, they may continue to make sacrifices, but allow the resentment to build to intolerable levels.

Another related dynamic is that of parents who distance themselves from their children through abuse, drawing the children's hatred, and in the bargain confirming themselves as loathsome characters. They may have themselves been abused in their own families of origin and have been blamed for it. They turn themselves

*Portions of this chapter previously appeared in Allen, 2001.

into monsters, possibly as a way of proving to themselves and their family that they deserved whatever mistreatment they received. A sexually abusing father may one minute tell her daughter, as Benjamin (1993) described, that she is the light of his life, and in the next breath tell her she is a filthy, seductive whore. At times parents may portray themselves as particularly reprehensible by seeming to be proud of the abuse they have heaped on to their children.

Saying that the parents of patients with BPD have such conflicts, however, is more of a description than an explanation. How and why are the conflicts created in the first place? To better understand how such a state of affairs comes to be, we must trace the origins of the conflict. This understanding of the genesis of the conflict can then be used in treatment to help patients find something redeeming about their parents, so that they can later discuss abuse issues with the parents without attacking them.

I have been constructing genograms (McGoldrick & Gerson, 1985) with BPD patients and their parents over the years, and have seen a number of patterns that may explain the origins of the parenting conflict. I now briefly list some of the major ongoing life events and issues that I have catalogued that may lead to extreme parental ambivalence. Before proceeding, the reader should keep in mind an important caveat: The issues to be described are extremely common in the general population. In and by themselves, they are in no way sufficient to produce a degree of dysfunction high enough to create psychopathology in the children of the family. Rather, through a process described elsewhere (Allen, 1988), they become greatly amplified by some combination of the family's historical experiences and idiosyncratic individual characteristics within that family. In the section that follows the description of the patterns, I describe in detail three case examples that are illustrative of the entire process.

First, gender issues continue to be a major source of discord in our culture. People feel torn between the desire to "have it all" and the desire to simplify their lives through the old gender-based division of labor within the family. Couples may require two incomes to even survive, yet feel guilty if they do not have children or stay home with them. These feelings may be amplified if they pursue a career in a field that expects long work hours and is not family friendly.

Women, on whom childcare responsibilities traditionally fall, are especially vulnerable to being torn apart by these conflicting priorities. Being caught between conflicting desires may make them resentful of their children for at times making their work lives so complicated, but then guilty about their resentment. Such conflicts and ambivalence can be exacerbated and magnified by the behavior of other family members. Say, for example, that a career woman's husband falls victim to unemployment. If she had been raised in a family composed mainly of highly energetic and intelligent yet traditional wives and mothers who were secretly envious of her career, she might get criticized relentlessly if she makes her husband take over more parenting duties, or just as much if she does not.

Second, untimely deaths in the family may create ambivalence over the parenting role. One grandparent of a patient had lost 10 out of 11 children to disease; the eleventh was the parent of a BPD patient. The grandmother was overprotective of the mother but at the same time avoided closeness for fear of the pain of losing yet another child. When the mother grew up and left home, the grandmother became depressed. My patient was then given up as a child to the care of the grandmother to help fill the void.

Third, financial reverses and chronic illnesses—including mental illnesses—may turn the joy of raising children into a frightful burden, both emotionally and financially, and thereby generate parental ambivalence. Interestingly, the presence of bipolar disorder—with which BPD is often confused—in a parent may lead to the very chaos in families that generates BPD behavior in children. Children in such a family are at risk both biologically for bipolar disorder and environmentally for BPD.

Fourth, ambivalence over religious or cultural values concerning childbearing, child rearing, and filial responsibilities may lead to parental ambivalence. Examples include:

1.   The Roman Catholic emphasis on large families in a day and age when children cost a small fortune to raise may lead parents to follow the church rules but be extremely unhappy about the results.

2.   Children, often the eldest female in a traditional family, may be called on to take care of younger siblings. In doing so they are often forced to give up exciting adolescent activities in which their peers at school indulge. The result may be that they become

identified with the caretaker role yet resentful of it. When they leave home and have families, this history may lead them to resent their own children.

3. The eldest male in a family may be called on to take over the family business in a career he happens to hate; the costs incurred in raising children may lead to continuing family pressure to keep the business going when he wants out.

A fifth issue involves parent–child role reversals. If adults in the family become incapacitated for whatever reason, and the children are therefore called on to take over heavy adult responsibilities prematurely, the children may become resentful in a manner analogous to that of the eldest female in a traditional family described earlier. Such individuals often describe this state of affairs with statements such as "I never got to be a kid." A similar situation occurs when parents who were infantilized by their own families of origin appear to be unable to take care of themselves. Their children then try to fill the power vacuum and take care of them before really being equipped to do so.

Last, when a couple has a child to try to "save the marriage," the child then becomes the reason that the parents must continue in a miserable relationship. The resentment within the marital dyad becomes symbolized by the child whose presence was supposed to make the relationship better, but instead has led to the continuation of the same old marital misery.

EXAMPLES OF FAMILY HISTORIES OF PATIENTS WITH BPD OR BPD TRAITS

Case 3-A was a woman in her mid-30s who presented with chronic dysthymia throughout her adult life and a marked tendency to get involved with controlling and violent alcoholic men. When she was still a teenager, she had been pressured by her family to marry a "nice" man whom she did not love. Later she became the first person in her family to get a divorce.

She began having affairs during her marriage, and after her divorce she continued a series of relationships with the aforementioned volatile and dangerous men. These men would often be hyper-jealous and forbid her to go out when they were not present.

It could not be said that she did not give them cause for concern; when she did go out, she would invariably sleep with other men.

Her family, particularly her mother, persistently and mercilessly criticized her for destroying her marriage. They believed it had been the one good relationship in her life. The patient was frequently told that she would go to hell because of the divorce. The family also provocatively maintained a very active and public relationship with the patient's exhusband.

Additionally, the mother vacillated between blaming the patient and then herself for a variety of other family problems. The mother's blame-shifting and guilt-inducing statements included, "You pick dangerous men just like your father;" "I know I was a bad mother; I did the best I could"; and "I know what it's like being on the bottom; if it weren't for the love of my kids, I would have killed myself." The mother also badgered the patient about not going to church; the patient felt like she did not deserve to be there.

The father had died when the patient was in her early 20s. As alluded to in the mother's comments, he was an extremely violent and controlling man who severely beat all the members of the family, extensively cheated on his wife, and drank to excess. Episodically, he would disappear for days at a time and leave his wife and kids with only a small amount of money on which to survive. He had told the patient over and over when she was a child that she was stupid and would never amount to anything, yet he turned to her first for help when he became sick and was dying.

When the patient was growing up, both parents kept her at home in almost cloistered isolation, much as her future boy friends would try to do later in her life. She was almost never allowed to go out except to go to school and church. However, she was allowed, over her mother's rather faint objections, to spend time with her father and his boisterous friends. Both parents had come from a highly restrictive Fundamentalist Christian background, where such things as dancing and music—not to mention drinking and adultery—were forbidden. Later, after the father had died, the mother stated that the reason she did not leave the father was because her religious beliefs forbid divorce. In actual fact, ironically, their church did allow for divorce in cases of adultery; the mother's marriage obviously would have qualified.

When a boy from a religious family expressed interest in 3A, her parents began to pressure her to marry him. For reasons that became clear as therapy progressed, the mother seemed to me to be hoping that marriage to this boy would prevent 3A from following in her footsteps. Early in therapy, the patient described herself as an unreasonable, adulterous monster who treated her husband horribly. As therapy progressed, however, the patient admitted that her husband routinely neglected the patient and their child and avoided sex with her almost completely. His family treated her like dirt, and he never defended her. He not only knew about the patient's affairs, he had no objections to them. Interestingly, one of the patient's siblings set her up with some the men with whom she had extramarital relationships.

The patient's mother seemed oblivious to the problems in the patient's marriage, partially because the patient rarely complained about them. When the patient finally decided to leave her husband, the mother promised her financial assistance; when the time arrived, the mother suddenly reneged.

In gathering family history, the larger picture began to emerge. The paternal grandfather was a stern minister who hypocritically had a second whole family with a woman with whom he was having an affair. Between his two "wives" he had a horde of children, all of whom he supported financially. Analogously, the patient's father helped support some of his nieces and nephews. This was part of the reason he was so stingy with giving the patient's mother money to live on. The grandfather was also violent, beating all of his children and some of his grandchildren.

The mother's family was remarkably similar. Her father was a Bible-thumping minister and a bootlegger; he would vacillate between a religious persona and a wild man persona. He would have frequent affairs. Additionally, he would often go out drinking with the mother's wild alcoholic sister. In parallel with the patient's history, this sister was the one who introduced the mother to her dangerous future husband. The patient's mother as a young woman was supposedly sheltered much like the patient. However, she sneaked out of the house to go out with her future husband; they went to bars together. The patient's maternal grandmother was a prescription drug abuser who slept in a separate room from the grandfather.

While overtly critical of the patient's divorce, the patient's mother and siblings exhibited subtle signs that they admired the patient for getting out of a bad relationship—something the mother had been unable to do. As mentioned, the mother had initially offered to help finance the patient's separation from her husband. On another occasion the mother gave the patient money to help her get out of an abusive relationship. One sibling even overtly admitted admiration for the patient's decision to get a divorce, but would nonetheless be critical of the patient in front of the mother. The siblings told one another that they wished the mother would leave her current husband, who was also extremely controlling.

The patient's role in her family was a combination of savior avenger, and spoiler. She would get out of bad relationships, thereby allowing the mother to vicariously live through her independence, only to jump right into another bad relationship. This helped her mother to justify her own stance against divorce. She punished her abusive boyfriends—as the mother was unable to punish her abusive husband—by frustrating their efforts to protect her and by cheating on them. The patient regulated her mother's guilt. Mirroring her mother's oscillation between blaming herself and then the patient for the family's problems, 3A would blame the mother for her problems when the mother seemed to need to feel guilty, but would blame herself when the mother started to feel *too* guilty.

Case 3-B (Allen, 2001) was a married female in her mid-30s who came to therapy complaining of recently worsening depression dating back to early childhood. She also complained of chronic irritability and anger, a history of leaving jobs whenever she became successful and feeling cut off from her family of origin.

The patient had a history of being seriously neglected as a young child. She was often kept locked up in her room when not at school, not taken to doctors when she was ill, and occasionally not even given food. She believed that her father hated her because had always seemed uncomfortable in her presence. When he did talk to her he tended to be verbally abusive. The mother often pushed the patient to excel in various activities but then stop her from participating just as she was about to achieve recognition. This seemed to parallel the patient's later tendency to push herself to high levels of achievement and then bail out when she was starting to do well.

The patient had moved to another city after she got married to her husband. The mother maintained contact with the patient after she left home, but her interactions with the patient were often limited to stereotypical interactions such as sermonizing about the evils of the outside world or formal Bible readings. The patient's older sister, who seemed to be the favorite, continued to live near the parents and was now spending a great deal of time looking after the parents, especially since the mother had become ill and physically incapacitated.

Sporadically, the patient would get a series of long distance telephone calls from her mother—sometimes several in a single day. During the calls, the mother would be alternately clinging or critical. On those occasions when the patient made a call to the parents, the father would almost never talk to her. If he happened to answer the phone, he would give the phone immediately to the mother.

Both grandmothers were bright and athletic women who had been deserted by their husbands. The paternal grandfather was a gambler who had frequently gambled away the family's food money before finally leaving them altogether. When he left, his wife was saddled with a large family of children and a large debt. The father's mother handled this situation by living with and being supported by her older children, while simultaneously pulling away from and ultimately neglecting her younger children. The patient's father was the youngest child. As he grew older, his mother seemed to want him to look after her but then rebuffed his efforts to help the family. This is an excellent example of the genesis of the "little man" role.

The maternal grandfather was a rake and a bohemian who eventually came to a bad end. The patient's mother had excelled in a number of endeavors as a child. Due to a lack of funds caused by her father's desertion, however, the maternal grandmother abruptly stopped the mother from continuing to pursue her talents. Nonetheless, the grandmother would act as if she were upper class and continued to expect achievement from her children. This pattern was probably the origin of the start–stop dynamic seen in both the patient and her mother.

In their youth, both parents were wild and rebellious. The mother in particular engaged in risky behavior. She eventually wound up, rather unjustly, in jail because of her nontraditional activities. Later, after the birth of their first child, the parents suddenly adopted a severely restrictive fundamentalist religion. They tried to keep their children away from the media but they read widely, ostensibly to know what material to keep away from their children.

Over the years, the mother gradually went from being very athletic and active to being extremely sickly and incapacitated. She would then badger her husband to take care of her every need. When he tried, the mother never seemed pleased with his efforts. I suggested to the patient that the mother was recreating his earlier experiences with his own seemingly needy, help-rejecting mother. The father viewed taking care of his wife as his sacred mission in life.

As the patient went through adolescence, the mother alternated between continuing to rein the patient in and looking the other way when she engaged in nonreligious behavior. The patient was continually lectured about the evils of sex, although she was allowed to have boys come to her room unchaperoned. The result was that 3B was never comfortable with sex even after she married. Interestingly, her husband, like her father, isolated himself much of the time. He rarely approached the patient for sex and never complained when she expressed a lack of interest. Actually, he thought sex vulgar. His parents believed in the same fundamentalist religion that the patient's parents subscribed to, and his father had isolated himself from his mentally ill wife, not unlike both his son and the patient's father.

This case illustrates a variation on the borderline role seen in families in which the neglect polarity predominates. The mother's occasional barrage of phone calls betrayed the fleeting presence of the overinvolvement polarity. Spoiling responses were present but were not a salient part of the patient's clinical picture; the patient functioned more in the role of a savior with a double bind on achievement. She would succeed in areas in which the mother would have excelled were it not for the unfortunate behavior of the maternal grandfather, but then pull back. The patient's father and sister mostly took up management of the mother's help-rejecting neediness. This, combined with her father's distancing behavior, freed the patient up somewhat to live her own life apart from her family of origin. She nonetheless did not feel she was free.

Case 3-C was an interesting case of a woman in her early 40s whose family dynamics seemingly met most of the characteristics that, according to the theory presented in this book, might be expected to produce a child with BPD. Although she did exhibit several BPD traits from time to time, they only appeared sporadically and for brief periods. She presented mostly in the role of the defective: Her somatic problems led to a referral to me from her internist. Her physician strongly suspected that her chronic medical condition was being exacerbated by psychological distress. For reasons that will become clear shortly, I believe that her medical illness obviated the need for her to engage in overt spoiling behavior. Her parents would get angry with her merely for being ill, and would often abandon her whenever she was.

At the time I first interviewed her, she was in the hospital. On initial encounter, she was as pleasant as pleasant could be, and quite cooperative. On inquiring about recent stresses in her life, I learned that she was on the verge of filing for divorce. By coincidence, her husband happened to call in the middle of the consultation. The change in her demeanor was astonishing; she seemed to suddenly change from Dr. Jeckyl into Mr. Hyde. She lambasted her husband in the nastiest, most biting manner imaginable, raking him over the coals for his lack of attentiveness and help. As soon as the phone call was over, she immediately turned back into the pleasant Dr. Jeckyl.

The husband had an amiable exterior, but would became very angry with his wife merely for being ill, was highly critical of her, and did not seem to want to take care of the children. The patient had had to quit work because of her own illness as well as the severe illnesses of her children—one of whom had died as a baby. As one might expect, she was constantly worried about her remaining children, but would not let her husband help her with their complicated medical regimen. She had reason not to trust him; he would never perform the regimen quite correctly.

The patient's parents were of more help with the children than the husband, but inconsistently. They would offer to take care of the children; indeed, they would get angry with the patient if she did not ask them to baby sit. Whenever she needed their help the most, however, they would abruptly leave for a vacation property they owned several hours away. This pattern became even more pronounced during the patient's divorce. Oddly, they encouraged the patient to purchase a house that was more than she could afford. When she tried to go back to work so she could pay for it, they would leave town just when the patient was scheduled for important job interviews. The patient had no one she could trust to take care of her children's medical needs besides the parents, and therefore she would have to cancel the interviews. When the patient complained, the parents would protest that they had other things they had to do. Those things were usually either trivial or something that could easily have waited.

The parents' seeming anger about their daughter's and grandchildren's illnesses and their passive–aggressive responses were, as usual, explained by their experiences with their own families of origin. The maternal grandmother had been severely ill with potentially life threatening conditions throughout the mother's childhood. The maternal grandparents had also lost a child to disease. The maternal grandfather was completely overwhelmed by the illnesses in the family and probably felt helpless and inadequate. At times he would get angry with his wife; most of time he was depressed and nearly nonfunctional. This created a power vacuum that lead to a role reversal in which the mother became her own mother's primary caretaker.

The mother was quite bright and had earned a scholarship to college. She was afraid to go, however, because she did not know who would look after her sick mother. Her mother, seeing the quandary, insisted that she go off and get her education. The patient's grandmother then turned to the mother's older sister for help. This aunt, who was married, soon thereafter divorced her husband and spent more time devoted to taking care of the grandmother.

On the father's side, the core issue was a gender conflict-based case of hypochondria in the paternal grandmother. For reasons we were never able to trace, the maternal grandmother emigrated from Europe alone as a young teenager. After coming to the United States, she worked all her life and in fact ran her own successful business. She married and then divorced several husbands, having children with all of them. The patient's father was the youngest child and quite a bit younger than his siblings were. The siblings had all left home as soon as they could because of their mother's distancing behavior.

Despite in reality being counterdependent and very powerful at work, the grandmother would present herself to the outside world and to her children as a very helpless, ill woman who was dependent on everyone to take care of her. Because she had driven away her husbands and other children, the role of caretaker fell to the patient's father. He resented it because he felt with good reason that his mother was a hypochondriac, but would dutifully come to her to help whenever he was called. His wife, the patient's mother, assisted him in this effort.

One habit of the paternal grandmother that was particularly irksome was her tendency to fall ill just when the patient's family was packed up and ready to leave for a vacation. They would usually have to cancel the trip. The parents' anger over this last behavior was expressed indirectly in their sudden urge to leave town whenever their daughter needed them the most.

Families such as the three presented in these case examples do at times try to talk about the problematic relationship patterns in an attempt to change them. Unfortunately, such attempts often create further discord and dissension, leading family members to avoid direct discussions of family dynamics. Nonetheless, because of the salience of the problems, they continue to be discussed obliquely. An understanding of the peculiarities of interpersonal communication in families of BPD patients can help a therapist to better understand the underlying family dynamics. In the next chapter, we look at dysfunctional communication in the families of BPD patients.

4

Metacommunication In BPD Families

Human communication between intimates is notoriously elliptical even in highly open and insightful families. Intimates share a common history that allows them to refer to events and relationship variables implicitly. They do not have to recount everything that has happened before that pertains to the conversation, nor precisely define everything that they say. If they had to do so, a simple conversation would take forever. Additionally, as much can be communicated by what is unsaid as by what is said (Tyler, 1978). The past history of the relationship and its entire context therefore permeates and colors everything that is said.

The therapist is not privy to all of this information; therefore the therapist must understand a lot about the background of the relationships, and the background of the family, to truly make sense out of what is being said in a family conversation. In Part II of this book we discuss how to draw out from the BPD patient accurate descriptions of family behavior and communication. In this chapter, we examine some of the unique problems inherent in the conversations of families that produce offspring with BPD.

Metacommunication is defined as communication by two or more individuals designed to discuss the nature of their relationship, or to discuss the rules that govern how the relationship is talked about. In families in the grip of severe conflict, the ability to calmly and tactfully discuss issues of power, role functioning, hurt feelings, possible misunderstandings, controversial behavior, and so forth is essential for establishing mutual understanding and engaging in effective relationship problem-solving. Unfortunately, this type of reasoned conversation does not happen very often in families that produce offspring that exhibit BPD. As we see in Part II of this book, the goal of systems-oriented psychotherapy is to teach the patient how, and to motivate them to, effectively metacommunicate with their family members in a context in which unpleasant reactions to metacommunication have previously been the norm. This is done with the further goal of altering dysfunctional interactions that reinforce the patient's self-destructive behavior.

FAMILY ARGUMENTS IN PATIENTS WITH BPD

From time to time, family members in those families with a son or daughter with BPD do try to talk about issues and resolve them. However, several problems inherent in their metacommunicative strategies routinely pop up that interfere with the achievement of mutual understanding and conflict resolution. The combination of the parents' high role-function ambivalence, their vicarious but covert identification with their children's behavior, and natural human defensiveness and shame invariably lead to this failure.

A common characteristic of families with a member who exhibits BPD is that family members *mutually* invalidate one another. As we see here, this phenomenon is a by-product of the role-function ambivalence and confusion discussed in the last chapter. When any conflictual issue is brought up, individuals who are highly confused about who they are supposed to be in the world and how they are supposed to act in certain situations have great difficulty truly committing to any definitive position on the matter. Because they feel themselves wrong no matter what position they take, and expect criticism either way, they never feel nor sound too sure of themselves. They tend to avoid making any statements that clearly define their values in regard to the conflictual issue.

They usually attempt to steer clear of such a subject altogether, but because the role conflict is usually a central concern, it has a way of coming out anyway. In this context, conflicted individuals often try to communicate real but forbidden desires in such a manner as to allow them to disavow the statements later if necessary. In other words, in case the family reacts in the expected negative way, positions are stated in such as way as to allow individuals to claim that they were misunderstood. Even the claim that they were misunderstood may come out ambiguously because the individuals may feel the need to reverse themselves again later on.

The structure of all human language is such that ambiguity is quite easy to generate. Any sentence in any language can refer to a multitude of unclear referents, or can be interpreted in antithetical ways. Negative evaluations can come out positive and vice versa through changes in body language, tone of voice, or even choice of synonym. For example, almost any descriptor with a positive or a negative connotation has a synonym with the opposite valence. An optimist, for instance, can be called a Pollyanna. Another trick that is employed to create ambiguity is the use of unvoiced implications. Individuals imply something without stating it explicitly, thusly creating opportunities for plausible deniability of those implications at a later date. A complete discussion of the antithetical nature of language is beyond the scope of this book, but can be found elsewhere (Allen, 1991).

As we discussed in chapter 2, individuals invariably attempt to form an understanding of what other family members expect of them. When faced with extreme ambiguity, they will attempt to gain clarification. They may try to do so by paraphrasing what the other person has said to see if they can gain the other person's agreement that they had correctly understood it. However, when a child from a family that generates BPD behavior repeats back a definitive conclusion they have drawn about where a parent stands on a conflictual issue, a problem arises immediately.

The nature of this problem can best be understood through the use of a hypothetical example. Let us say that a mother is, unbeknownst to her daughter, ambivalent about gender-role functioning. Let us further postulate that Mom had secretly wished to become a professional, but that her family-of-origin had invalidated a career orientation in females. In response, she had elected to lived her life as a traditional housewife and mother, all the while being covertly unhappy about it. In this scenario, if the daughter attributes to her mother *either* a feminist *or* a traditionalist position on female career ambition, the daughter will come up against the *other* side of the mother's ambivalence.

No matter which way the daughter characterizes her concept of the mother's philosophy, the mother will become uncomfortable and will avoid definitively agreeing with her perceptions. The mother becomes uncomfortable with either attribution because of her own underlying conflict. Covertly, the mother has probably already invalidated her own true thoughts and feelings in the matter—in this case the idea that she has sacrificed a career she really wanted—as unacceptable. In the process of avoiding a confirmation of the daughter's attribution, she outwardly invalidates the daughter's perception of the mother's position on the issue.

Because the daughter gets invalidated no matter which attribution she makes, she ends up confused about where the mother really stands on the issue. More perniciously, she becomes unsure of her own observations on which her opinion was based, and may even question her own sanity. As we shall see shortly, the mother's behavior also ends up invalidating any decision that the daughter makes about what path to choose for herself.

If the daughter were to point out that the mother is giving out confusing or contradictory messages, the mother would naturally tend to get angry or defensive. She might deny that she is being contradictory, thusly invalidating the daughter's observations once again. The mother in this scenario can not acknowledge mixed feelings for fear of attack from her own spouse and family of origin, and she may also resent the implied accusation that she is not doing right by her daughter. The mother may feel the latter *in spite* of the fact that she may on the surface be knowingly distancing her daughter (that is, pushing the daughter away from her) through being difficult.

Distancing behavior from parents toward a child frequently results when the parents have a role conflict. The child's questions and his or her own need to make a decision about what role to play forces the parents to confront an issue that causes them great anxiety. They may become ambivalent over the child's very presence. For example, the mother in our hypothetical case may begin to feel that both she and her daughter would be better off if they were not exposed to each other for two reasons. First, the mother may feel that, because she is creating confusion for the daughter in the first place, the daughter would be freer to choose her own path without her. Second, although the daughter may be a source of vicarious gratification of the mother's ambition, she is also a constant reminder to the mother that the mother did not get to do what she really wanted to do. The mother will at times appear to be relieved when the daughter leaves.

Adding further to the mother's ambivalence and confusion about the presence of the child are two other factors. First, Mom has a natural bond with her child that makes an emotional cut off uncomfortable in its own right. Second, the mother may feel great shame that she has not been able to proceed with her desires against the apparent wishes of her own family of origin.

If the daughter were to say that she is planning to, say, go to law school, the mother might seem to discourage her, although in a typically ambiguous manner. This does not happen out of petty jealousy, although envy is certainly a factor. Because she herself was criticized for being too "masculine" when she talked about a career plan, the mother legitimately fears that others in the family and elsewhere might react negatively to her daughter's ambitions. If, on the other hand, daughter elects to forgo law school in order to get married, the mother will seem to discourage that as well. In this case, the negative reaction would also occur for two reasons. First, the mother would no longer be able to sublimate her own ambition through vicariously living through her daughter. Second and more important, she would want to spare her daughter from the disappointment that she herself had felt when she gave up her own ambitions.

No matter what the daughter say in regards to ambition and women, the mother ends up shooting a hole in it. Any idea the daughter has about her own career plans is therefore invalidated. This leads the daughter to be both unsure of her own sense of reality in regards to what the mother has said and confused about how she herself should proceed in regards to her career. This will lead, in turn, to her avoiding taking a clear-cut position on the issue herself.

Once this scenario has played out, what happens if the mother decides to bite the bullet, so to speak, and tries to discuss the issue with her daughter? What happens when the mother attempts to clarify the daughter's position? Because the daughter is now reluctant to declare herself, the daughter will end up invalidating the mother's observations in exactly the same way that the mother had invalidated the daughter. This *mutual* invalidation leads to the *mutual* reinforcement of the dysfunctional relationship pattern by both daughter and mother as they try to read one another's intentions. I have termed this process *cross motive reading*.

Further invalidation of the BPD individual comes about through the distancing behavior described previously. Because distancing behavior is performed ambivalently by the distancer, language is once again used ambiguously. For example, a mother may admire her daughter in some way, but make it sound as if she were critical about the behavior that she really admires.

A good illustration of this process occurred in a conversation between a nurse and her mother. The mother was discussing the daughter's rather assertive stance toward the mostly male physicians with whom the daughter worked. The mother said, "I can't *believe* you talk to doctors that way!" The patient took this to mean that the mother believed that she should not engage in this behavior. In one sense this was an accurate assessment of the mother's view, but it was only part of the whole truth. The mother indeed was worried that the daughter might get fired. Such would have been the case during earlier times, when the mother was younger. As it turned out, however, the mother was *also* expressing covert admiration for the nurse's bravery, assertiveness, and feminist leanings. What Mom had difficulty believing was that the patient had nerve that the mother lacked. Her critical tone of voice obscured the admiration. The actual lexical content of the comment has no positive or negative valence at all.

Another ambiguous distancing statement, made by a traditional mother to her highly accomplished daughter, was, "I'm glad I did not have a second daughter; I couldn't handle two like you!" The patient naturally assumed that this meant she was so awful that the mother wished she had never been born. Covertly, however, the mother was referring to *her own* difficulty seeing her daughter get to do what she had never been able to do. What the mother had trouble "handling" was her own envy. The way it came out was meant to distance the patient, but in the process it also ended up invalidating all of the daughter's accomplishments. In doing so, the comment was invalidating the *personhood* of the daughter, who began to question her entire self-worth.

In these examples, comments were made that appeared to apply to one member of a parent–child dyad, but actually applied to both of them. The identification with and the living through of children by their parents is the source of the so-called "boundary disturbances" described by analytic writers in their discussions of the phenomenology of BPD. Because of identification, the parent may appear to be talking about the offspring while really thinking covertly about himself or herself. Most patients with BPD do not realize that this is taking place because the parents' self-referential thoughts are not directly expressed. Episodically, however, the parent may suddenly launch into a discussion about his or her own experiences. At times, in fact, the patient with BPD may never be quite sure who is really being talked about. After a while the patient wonders, "Is this thought really coming from me, or am I parroting what I've been told? And what exactly is it that I have been told?" Identify confusion becomes part of the patient's symptom picture as these confusing conversations are internalized and incorporated into cognitive role relationship schemata.

In the following excerpt from a conversation between a mother and a patient with BPD (Case 4-A), I believe that the mother's covert anger over how she herself was treated as a child colored the whole conversation. This led to boundary confusion and invalidation. The mother also invalidates herself, as evidenced by the italicized portion of the excerpt. The reader should note the point in the conversation during which the mother without warning shifts into talking about her own childhood. The context of the conversation was an attempt by the patient to discuss long verbal harangues by the mother that the patient had been subjected to as a child, and that were continuing into the present. In the transcript, M is the mother, and Pt is the patient:

M: … and then things that you remember yourself, you don't
     know the other side of it and your side of it—either.
Pt: What do you mean I don't know the other side of it?
M: Well I mean you know one person's side. Like somebody
     did something to you, but you don't know what you did
     to that person. So … and neither does anybody else.
Pt: What have I … What have I ever done to anyone?
M: I don't know!
Pt: I don't either.
M: *I mean, and if I did know, I don't know it now.*
Pt: Oh [as if enlightened]. So, did I do something to some-
     body?
M: No! Not that I know of.

Pt: [silent]

M: I mean if you were scolded. You say, "Well I remember the time you spanked me." Well, or whatever. That's stupid but, whatever. Wha- what did you do to provoke that?

Pt: [long silence].

M: Do you know that? No. It's trivia.

Pt: I pretty much remember any time there was ... I mean ...

M: I don't remem – I don't remember what my brother did to me or my father or my mother or my friend or ... I mean, I don't know what causes things and what I did when I was younger or a teenager or ... I don't remember what I did to deserve that, you know what I'm saying?

Pt: Well, did I ever do anything really bad?

M: No. I don't know. Maybe you did, I don't even remember. And if you did, so what?

Pt: Well, wouldn't you remember?

M: No! 'cause it is not important to me.

Pt: Well I'd like to know if I did something bad.

M: I didn't say you did. I said, "*If* you did."

Pt: Well, I know I'm saying ... (exasperated sigh). I don't understand what you're talking about, I guess.

M: (pause). I mean, who knows about that nonsense? Who knows how bad ... I was a bad little girl.

Another major issue that leads to ambiguous conversations in the families of patients with BPD is that of shame. Shame and the defensiveness that it generates are a major source of the denial so often seen in families where child abuse is an issue. The denial, of course, is yet another form of invalidation. The victims are essentially being told that they have a very faulty memory because the abuse did not happen or was not as severe as they think. Denial occurs routinely even in situations where the perpetrator has no fear of being punished for the behavior; therefore I do not believe that avoidance of prosecution is the primary motive for denial in these situations.

Incest perpetrators and child abusers who admit to such behavior may at times cover up shameful feelings by going to the opposite extreme. They may act and talk as if they are perversely proud of their behavior. Like denial, this is really a cover up. They know as well as anyone that what they did was bad and that others think they are monsters, but they will deny that they know this.

The following excerpt of a conversation between a father and his adult daughter with BPD (Case 4-B) shows instances of both elliptical references to abuse and some statements that came close to being an admission of past wrongdoing. Of interest is that the quasi-admissions, which are italicized, seem almost sneaked into the conversation.

In the conversation, the daughter had been complaining about both the father's critical nature and the way he made her do chores when she was an adolescent. To a casual observer, it looked as if the daughter was being absurdly critical of having been asked to do work around the house. In the excerpt, the father even says that it is the daughter rather than he who would appear unreasonably critical to the outside world. Background information that, if known, would likely change the opinion of the outside world was alluded to but not said. In an earlier session when the father was not present, the patient had alleged to the therapist that one of her "chores" was the provision of sexual favors.

She refused to bring this up explicitly in the conjoint meeting. She did, however, become quite angry when the father complimented her on losing weight. This, of course, was reference to her body. In the transcript, F is the father.

F: People know that I think the world of you and I love you but I can't condone some of the things you've done.

Pt: [flashes anger] Hey, I don't condone some of the things that you do and you've done.

F: Well, obviously you don't; obviously you don't. That's just life you know [averts his eyes].

Pt: Yeah, yeah, that's true.

F: I do notice that you've lost some weight. I think that's admirable.

Pt: [sarcastically] Thank you, father, I appreciate that pat on the back.

F: Is that the only pat you got in your life? You sound like you're starved for admiration.

Pt: There is no admiration from you, only condemnation and judgment.

F: That's not true. I think if anyone observed any condemna-
     tion in the two of us talking, it'd be from your standpoint.
Pt: Oh yeah, 'cause I have a lot of rage that won't go away.
F: It's called the blame game. You blame ...
Pt: No, it's not called the blame game.
F: You blame things that you've done ...
Pt: I can not resolve this screwed up family relationship.
F: I can not *blame the stuff that I've done in my life that I'm not
     proud of* on my mother. I mean, I shouldn't do that.
Pt: Heavens, no, your mother is blameless.
F: I mean, *I've made a lot of mistakes* and I don't go around
     blaming everybody.
Pt: I don't sit around and I don't either. I resent the fact that
     you won't face reality.
F: What reality won't I face? Name one thing.
Pt: Just what I referred to as a child—the responsibility that I
     had to carry.

One last crucial element in understanding conversations between
patients with BPD and their families involves certain key phrases
used by family members that trigger rage reactions in the patient. As
anyone familiar with BPD knows, rage can be triggered suddenly—
and seemingly unexpectedly—in these patients. Family members as
well as therapists often accuse patients with BPD of misinterpret-
ing harmless statements as hostile or overreacting to the most mi-
nor of slights.

At times, patients with BPD do in fact put on a phony display of
anger as part of spoiling behavior. Some of the time, however, the
anger is very real and quite understandable. Once the full context of
the patient's relationship history is understood, it becomes frighten-
ingly clear that the patient is reacting as any normal person might.
The innocuous-sounding words and phrases are, in the family context, actually "fighting words." Because the words have become so
noxious, patients with BPD are often primed to explode even when
the words are used in other more benign contexts.

For example, one patient (Case 4-C) went into a rage when her
mother used the phrase "my precious children." To a casual observer, this response was irrational. The casual observer would not
know, however, that as a child the mother had routinely whipped

the patient mercilessly with an iron cord, and on one occasion had forced her to eat feces out of her baby brother's diaper. The logic of the patient's apparently irrational response was this: "If we were so precious to you, how could you have mistreated us like that?"

The same patient erupted when the mother said to her, "You've always been so happy and outgoing." In truth, the patient had been depressed and socially withdrawn for quite some time. The mother's statement was, to the patient, an invalidation of her entire reality.

CASE I-A: A TRANSLATION

Now that we have reviewed some important aspects of metacommunication in families that produce offspring with BPD, let us at last return to the argument between the mother and the violent daughter (Case 1-A) that was presented in chapter 1. I will translate it into terms that can be understood and dealt with more effectively by a therapist.

As mentioned, understanding a conversation between two individuals with a long history behind them requires much knowledge about the background of the relationship. In this case, I received direct confirmation of something the patient had told me because the mother came to see me for therapy after I was no longer treating the daughter.

Every time the mother came to therapy she would, despite being a very efficient, in-charge career woman during the day, come into the office and, as if on cue, begin to cry incessantly. Her demeanor in my office was quite different from her demeanor at work. She looked quite depressed. Clearly, the daughter had seen much of this behavior. I recalled that the daughter had frequently complained to me that her mother was very depressed. The daughter had in fact come to believe that the only thing that seemed to get the mother out of her depression was being angry with her daughter.

This view was reinforced by other contextual factors. One was the mother's gift of the car that did not run. The car is an ideal symbol of the "go away—I need you" dynamic in families of BPD patients. The daughter thought that, in order to be stable, the mother really wanted her to stick around. The patient felt herself to be needed as a sort of punching bag that helped the mother to distract herself from her depression. Her view of the mother was further reinforced by the way the mother avoided doing things, such as filling out college aid forms and pursuing her exhusband for child support, which might have led to the patient becoming less dependent on her.

Provocatively, the mother's anger often took the form of criticism of the daughter's lack of independence—something the behavior mentioned earlier seemed to preclude. When the girl actually *was* independent, the mother seemed to become more unstable. This aggravating double bind led the patient to develop a second idea about the needs of the mother. The mother, in the patient's view, also needed her to be violent. Why else would mom stick her nose in the daughter's face in the middle of the girl's rage? The patient *literally* thought her mother was asking for it, and in fact, needed it. The mother seemed to be guilty all the time; perhaps she felt that she deserved to be punished for some unknown transgression.

The apparent switches in subject during the argument from the daughter's school problems to the mother's sloppiness to the daughter's drug use were not really subject switches at all, as all of these subjects were related to the family dynamics. The girl was trying to give her mother a message in a typically ambiguous manner. The message was this: The daughter did not become independent in a healthy way because, the daughter believed, it would adversely affect the mother's mental health. The mother's mental condition was typified by the way the mother let the house go.

The daughter's use of drug dealing to "support" herself was actually a pseudo-move toward independence. Its purpose was to give the mother yet another vehicle by which she could continue their relationship as it then existed. She *knew* that the mother would criticize her for it. Nonetheless, when the mother did so, it reinforced her view that the mother did not want her to gain financial independence. The mother should have said, but did not, that she was glad the patient wanted to support herself, but that it was the *way* the daughter chose to do so that was problematic.

If the daughter better understood the mother's apparent double messages as a reflection of the mother's *internal* conflict, instead of as the mother's vehicle for destroying the girl's own independence, she might have been more empathic toward the mother's position. She might then respond with less acting out and more conversation. If the mother and daughter could somehow learn to metacommunicate about the mother's ambivalence over allowing her child grow up, then the mother might become more aware of exactly how she is adversely affecting the daughter. She can then stop acting in ways that reinforce the daughter's acting out. The daughter would then feel free to grow up; her spoiling behavior would begin to go away because it would no longer be reinforced by the mother's disqualification of individuated behavior.

This then can become the primary goal of systems-informed individual psychotherapy with adult patients with BPD: Teaching the patient about the family dynamics and their role in it, about how to be empathic rather than quite so angry, and about how to constructively discuss patterns with reluctant family members rather than acting out. The psychotherapy of BPD is the subject of Part II.

II

Unified Therapy
of Patients With Borderline
Personality Disorder

5

Rationale for the Treatment Approach

Unified therapy (Allen, 1988, 1991, 1993, 2001) is an integration of psychodynamic, cognitive-behavioral, and family systems theories and treatment techniques. Ideas and techniques from experiential and existential therapies are also incorporated into the therapy. The treatment is designed for individual psychotherapy with adults from the age of 23 to 48 years old exhibiting self-destructive or self-defeating behavior patterns, chronic affective symptomatology, or chronic family discord. One or two of these features may be the initial focus of the patient's chief complaint; in my experience, however, if one or two of these manifestations are present, the other or others eventually reveal themselves. The theory behind the treatment predicts that it will not be effective for younger individuals, for whom direct family therapy may be necessary. The treatment is particularly useful for the treatment of cluster B and C personality disorders, with the exception of antisocial personality disorder. This part of the book focuses on the specific application of unified therapy theories and techniques to the psychotherapy of BPD.

To reiterate, the basic premise behind the unified therapy theory of the creation of borderline personality disorder is that the parents in the patient's family of origin have a severe psychodynamic conflict over the parenting role. This conflict leads them to give out double messages to one or more of their children. The message that the focused-on child receives is a mixture of "I need you desperately" and "I hate you, go away." These conflicting messages create conflictual role-performance demands on the patient in regards to autonomy and independence from the parents. Although some families of BPD patients are consistently highly enmeshed with them or become consistently cut off from them, the usual clinical picture is that of families that oscillate between hostile over and underinvolvement with the BPD patient. A push–pull is created in which the child becomes a sort of yo-yo, pulling away and then being drawn back in to the family chaos. The mixed messages also reinforce spoiling-type responses in the children, no matter their age.

The parental behaviors that trigger borderline-type responses occur at variable frequencies and intensities, and are often mixed in with a variety of additional double messages over other issues. This process creates the wide variety of clinical presentations of patients with BPD. Parents or other family system leaders are thought, for genetic reasons, to be the most potent of all environmental influences in both shaping and reinforcing role-relationship schemata in all human beings. Because of this power, the parental behavior that triggers dysfunctional behavior in children does not have to occur frequently, although it often does, in order to have a major effect.

This parental behavior operates in a manner analogous to what learning theorists term a *variable intermittent reinforcement schedule.* This means that the parental behavior, although somewhat predictable, does not occur all the time, yet may happen at any time. Behavior reinforced on such a schedule has been noted by behaviorists to be extremely resistant to extinction. The person subject to the reinforcement continually and persistently tries for an expected response despite any initial lack of success in doing so because he or she never quite knows when the behavior *will* produce the response. The variable intermittent schedule is the reason gamblers keep pulling the lever on a slot machine although they are losing money. The machine pays off just often enough and unpredictably enough to keep the gambler hooked.

Observers who do not understand this process can be easily misled into forming opinions about patients with BPD and their families that are only partially valid. This can happen in at least three ways. First, because there are significant lulls in the "action," the problematic parental behavior may not be seen, even if the parents are observed for quite some time. A second way observers can be misled is when either the parent or the child purposely portrays himself or herself as the "villain" or the "victim," so that an observer gets a biased view of who exactly is misbehaving. In this scenario, the observer invariably overestimates the contribution of one player in the drama while seriously underestimating the contribution of the others.

Yet a third way observers may be misled is through the well-known borderline ruse of "splitting" others: The patient with BPD consistently acts like a victim with one set of interacting individuals while acting like the aggressor with another set. If the two groups do not discuss the basis of their observations with one another, they predictably line up for and against the patient. Implicitly they also line up for and against the patient's family members, who are also seen as either victims or aggressors. Unless one has a video camera operating on the patient and the family 24 hours a day, one can never be quite sure whether or not anybody's perception of the patterns in the family is completely accurate. We discuss later how to get passed "distortions" in the reports of patients with BPD to get a more accurate idea of what really transpires in the family interactions.

Because of the episodic yet pervasive nature of the behavior of patients with BPD, as well as their family members, these patients are particularly prone to be misdiagnosed by psychiatrists who do not spend much time with them. This is especially true if the psychiatrist does not know how to elicit from them accurate descriptions of themselves, others, and their interactions. In particular, short-lived mood symptoms stirred up by horrific family interactions are often thought to be both occurring "out of the blue" and lasting longer than they actually do. This leads to BPD patients being misdiagnosed as having "Bipolar II" disorder. We discuss evaluation procedures that prevent misdiagnosis later, along with a brief discussion of the use of psychiatric medications.

Before going on to describe the treatment methodology based on an understanding of family interactional sequences, I would first like to answer some potential objections to the conceptualization of BPD described in this book.

MODEL OF THE GENESIS OF BPD: CONTROVERSIES

First, I address the concept of the *double bind*. Because the unified therapy model posits a version of the double bind, and because the concept has a somewhat troubled history, some clinicians may see its inclusion as a weakness in the model. A double bind was first described in the early family therapy literature as a family pattern that includes four elements: The family members are "damned if they do" engage in certain behaviors and "damned if they do not" engage in those very same behaviors. They can not leave the family, nor can they comment on the bind that they are in.

Patients with conflictual behavior are, in my opinion, often victims of such binds. The patient with BPD, in particular, is clearly in a rather virulent version of a double bind. Because of severe parental role function ambivalence, BPD patients can neither differentiate nor stay enmeshed comfortably; no matter which way they go, they come up against the other side of the parents' ambivalence. If they try to "divorce" the family, they are subject to existential terror. If they point out the bind, they are met with disqualification and invalidation. They can neither be alone nor with others without anxiety. They can not function with the family or without them. As we shall see, if clients can get past the rather formidable defenses of the family and comment on the bind without being disqualified or invalidated, they can alter the dysfunctional relationship sequences that reinforce their self-destructive behavior and affective symptoms.

The idea that a family double bind might be a major contributor to psychopathology received a bad rap because double binding was initially observed in the families of schizophrenics, and was postulated by early family therapists to be the cause for that disorder. Although being placed in such a bind may exacerbate psychotic symptoms in an afflicted patient—double binds may possibly be one element that contributes to high "expressed emotion" in families—a double bind is certainly not a cause of psychosis. The families of schizophrenics, who later organized into the National Alliance for the Mentally Ill, were righteously indignant—and correctly so—about being directly blamed for what is now clearly known to be a central nervous system abnormality.

Double binding behavior in families is actually quite common. It is hardly limited to the families of schizophrenics. If the early family observers had brought in families of patients with other psychiatric diagnoses and compared them to families of patients with schizophrenia as well as individuals with no psychiatric disorders, they would have found this to be the case.

However, just because double binds do not cause psychosis, this does not mean that they do not contribute to other kinds of psychological problems. In particular, I believe personality disorders are reinforced by certain specific types of conflictual family-of-origin behavior that is highly prevalent in the families of patients with those various disorders. In 23 years of clinical experience, I have traced family relationship patterns and genograms in patients who exhibited a large variety of psychiatric disorders. The nature, extent, and severity of the patterns I described in Part I seem to be unique to the families of patients with BPD or BPD traits. On only one occasion did I find a patient with the disorder whose family did not seem to be conflicted over the patient's autonomy. Even then, I am not sure that I was being told the whole story. Of course, these are only personal observations that are subject to my own biases. Proof of these observations awaits further studies currently in progress.

Another potential objection to the idea that parental behavior sets in motion a chain of transactional events that culminate in the production of the manifestations of BPD involves the question of unaffected siblings. Some therapists have objected that all children in a household have been exposed to the same dysfunctional family interactions; therefore, if the interactions cause the disorder, all should be equally affected. Clearly this is not the case; only a small minority of such families have several children who all have the disorder.

The difficulty with this line of reasoning is that it presumes that parents interact with all of their children in approximately the same manner. This is also clearly not the case. Parents with ambivalence over the parental role may focus their entire conflictual behavior on one or perhaps two of their children, leaving the others relatively unscathed. In my experience, both the severity of dysfunction of a patient with BPD and the percentage of children in their families who share the disorder vary directly with two factors: the degree of the parents' ambivalence over the parenting role, and the severity of the family chaos that may be blamed on one or more children.

In families with several children, which child or children becomes the primary focus of the parents' conflict depends on a variety of factors. Certainly a child's innate temperament plays a role. A parent who really does not fully want to be a parent but who feels guilty about this impulse will react more problematically to an innately difficult child than to an easy child. The latter simply requires a lot less attention, whereas the former requires much more time. Additionally, the problems of a difficult child may feed into a parent's guilt over wishes to be free of family burdens. The parents may become concerned that perhaps their unacknowledged dislike for taking care of children is the cause of the child's problems. Hence, parents who are already feeling overburdened yet guilty will often feel guiltier with difficult children. In response, they often try to overcompensate by getting more involved with those children, which may then further increase their resentment over the parenting role. The difficult temperament of the child and the internal conflict of the parents feed off of one another, leading to more family conflict and chaos, and so forth. This interactional process confounds determinations of the contribution of genetics—which sets the thermostat for an individual's temperament—to personality pathology. The genetic contribution to personality will be discussed further shortly.

The other major factor that determines which child or children becomes "it" has to do with the natural similarities between particular children and the parents themselves, or between the children and other family members with whom the parents may have had a conflictual relationship. Parents are well known to both identify and counter-identify with their own children.

Say, for example, the mother is the oldest sister in a traditional family and had been required to give up her social life or college as a young woman in order to take care of her younger siblings. She then grows up and has children of her own, thrusting her back into the conflictual position. Because of identification, she might feel sorry for her oldest daughter and envious of her youngest daughter. Conversely, depending on the extent and severity of her resentment and her conflict over it, she might be harshest on the eldest daughter, who reminds her most of herself. Either way, the manner in which she interacts with each daughter will be completely different. Furthermore, if one of the daughters has physical or temperamental similarities to the mother's own mother, the mother might displace her repressed rage at her own mother on to that particular child. Because of the multiplicity of factors involved, determining the reasons why one child is the primary focus in any particular family is a speculative and difficult endeavor. Luckily, a completely accurate identification of these factors is not necessary for planning strategies for altering dysfunctional interactions. An educated guess will usually suffice.

I would now like to make a few points regarding the question of the genetic contribution to personality pathology. Estimates of the genetic contributions to behavior are generally made using twin and adoption studies. These studies have led to a statistical estimate known as *heritability*. Heritable, however, is not a synonym for genetic. Heretability estimates are based on phenotypes, not genotypes. Phenotype refers to the final external presentation of genetic processes, whereas genotype refers to the presence or absence of the actual genes themselves. Most genes in any organism are not expressed at any given time. They are turned on and off according to input from the external and internal environment of the body. Hence, a process like the one described earlier, in which genetic and environmental factors play off one another may lead to inflated heritability estimates that are not accurately reflective of true genetic differences.

Even if we use the somewhat inaccurate gauge of heritability for determining genetic contributions to personality traits, estimates of heritability on most personality traits range from 30% to 50%. This means that the majority of the variance is still explained by environmental factors. Consistent with the idea that children are not all treated alike by parents, it is usually the *unshared* environment that is thought to be of greater importance in determining traits than the shared environment (Paris, 1998).

When looking at heritability studies, three other points should be kept in mind. First, according to Livesay, Jang, Jackson, and Vernon (1993), heritability estimates of conduct disorder, self-harm, and insecure attachment are all below 35%. This means that strictly environmental factors are almost twice as important as heritable ones for those traits. Second, even when the heritability estimate of a trait is over 50%, such as with oppositionality, this only means that the child is *more likely* to be oppositional than another child who does not have this tendency. By no means is the child destined to be oppositional. Genetic factors that affect behavior determine a *range* of possible behaviors; the environment determines which behaviors *within* the range come to fruition. A good analogy is human speech patterns. Linguists have shown that there is a significant genetic contribution to these patterns, but whether one speaks Greek or Swahili is entirely determined by the environment.

Third and most important, phenotypic expression of behavior is context dependent. Even the most introverted of individuals displays extroverted behavior under some circumstances. Oppositional people are not *always* oppositional; they behave this way with certain other people in certain situations. Patients with BPD do not always act in a "borderline" fashion. I have had numerous opportunities to observe individuals I know to have been diagnosed with BPD when they did not know I was paying close attention to their behavior. This occurred during social situations when I was not their therapist. If I did not already have knowledge that they were self-mutilators, I would never have guessed that they were in a million years. Their behavior was pleasant and completely socially appropriate over extended periods of time.

On the other hand, some preliminary data from neuroscience studies has indicated that brain development and the patterns of the release of stress hormones may be adversely affected by ongoing traumatic stress, such as might be produced by living in an abusive and confusing environment. Parts of the brain important in social relationships, such as the hippocampus, may even show signs of atrophy (Siegel, 1999). This could indicate that some of the behavior of patients with BPD might be due to structural and functional neurophysiological abnormalities, especially if this defect is combined with the formation of cognitive schemata that lead to the assumption that the world is a hostile place.

It is therefore possible that the hyper-reactivity of BPD patients is due to some inherent deficit in affect regulation, although we do not know for sure that this is the case. The deficit, however, would be created by the interpersonal relationship atmosphere during childhood, rather than by a genetic deficit per se. However, studies using attachment theory show that the narratives that adults use to describe their own early family experiences can predict their child's attachment patterns before the child is even born (Siegel, 1999), and that attachment patterns can be quite different in a given child with each parent. These data show that the combination of the child's inborn temperament and the reactions of the parents to it can not entirely account for attachment patterns.

At this stage of our knowledge, it is quite possible that, given the right environmental input, any environmentally induced brain abnormalities in BPD may be reversible. Also, there is redundancy in the brain that might allow some functions to be "taken over" by other parts of the brain if one part is damaged. Even if it turns out that patients with BPD do in fact have a biological impairment in their ability to regulate affect, this does not necessarily mean that they have no capacity for learning how to do so. The biological substrate may only make it more difficult to those with the disorder than for those without.

BASIC PREMISES OF THE TREATMENT APPROACH

As we have seen, the unified therapy paradigm predicts that parents who are conflicted over their own choices in life, particularly when it comes to bearing and parenting children, will inadvertently induce their children to feed into their conflict. The children will end up reinforcing the parents' pre-existing conflictual role behavior. The children's behavior also provides the parents with a rationale for continuing to do whatever they are already doing.

The active role of future BPD patients in this process is induced when they are children but continues into their adulthood. As the process develops over time, the children's central nervous system continues to mature, and they go through the process of separation and individuation. They develop a much higher capacity for introspection and self-examination. In addition, as they mature they are exposed more and more to the culture outside of the family. In our individualistic western culture, the more pluralistic, ambient culture becomes increasingly influential on them. At some point during their lives, all neurologically intact human beings must begin to notice that other families around them do not all behave in the same ways. Sooner or later our culture induces all individuals to question themselves about whether their own behavior is really making them happy or unhappy. This simply must happen unless (with apologies to comedian Bill Mahre) they live alone in a cave and do not get cable. Cultures such as the old Soviet Union or present-day Iran that have tried to limit access to information about outside cultural norms and values have failed or are failing miserably.

Therefore, in my opinion, all individuals in an open culture develop to a point where continuing to play out particular role-relationship schemata becomes a choice. They may later engage in this behavior automatically and without thought, but at some basic level, it remains a choice. Granted, innate biological mechanisms make it extremely difficult to choose to give up such roles because doing so leads to existential terror. Although they may deny it, I believe that people continue to care about their families of origin no matter how miserably they have been treated by that family and no matter how little contact they may have. Nonetheless, existential anxiety per se is hardly lethal, and individuals have the choice to either continue or to stop playing out their family script even in its face.

In dysfunctional families, progeny often elect to continue to play out their script. They may occasionally try out new and different behaviors in an attempt to "help" their conflicted parents, but such attempts often fail. Because of their limited understanding of family dynamics, there usually seems to be no other viable option for them to maintain family homeostasis other than continuing to act as they have. To stop doing so often means disqualification or even exile from the entire family, and even worse, a family disaster of one sort or another.

From the position of younger members in a dysfunctional family, contradictory parental behavior is mystifying. The children usually come up with their own theory about it eventually, but most know that they really do not have a clue. There is simply no way for them to know that the family is functioning using rules that were designed to solve problems from an earlier generation. Neither can they intuit effective strategies for communicating so that they can get past their family's natural resistance to openly discussing conflictual issues.

Enter the therapist. Therapists who have studied psychology, psychotherapy, and family dynamics are aware of information about those subjects of which the average citizen is unaware. Armed with knowledge about how to interpret genograms, the therapist can help the patient understand and be empathic with troublesome parental behavior. The knowledgeable therapist can then help the patient learn how to harness that empathy in order to get past family denial and defenses, which in turn may allow the patient to effectively metacommunicate about and resolve problematic family interactions. The patient can learn that his or her role function behavior, although stabilizing the family in the short run, is actually backfiring and prolonging the family dysfunction. By helping the parents continue in their own conflictual roles, the patient with a personality disorder is actually helping the parents avoid facing and solving conflicts.

In unified therapy, it is not the job of the patient to "fix" the parents. However, by altering the way they approach the parents, patients can force the parents to alter troubling relationship patterns with them. If a discussion of family dynamics then helps the parents in their other problematic relationships, which it often does, all the better. That is not, however, the primary goal of treatment.

The therapist is paid for his or her knowledge of psychological and family functioning. Just as a lawyer is paid for what he or she knows, so is a therapist. The remainder of this book consists of a treatment manual designed to show how a therapist can accomplish six strategic goals with patients with BPD:

1. Frame the patient's chief complaint and current difficulties as a response to family of origin issues.
2. Gather information identifying interpersonal relationship patterns that cue self-destructive behavior.
3. Gather information about the patient's genogram for the purpose of understanding family misbehavior, so that the patient can develop empathy for targeted family members.
4. Make an hypothesis about both the patient's current role in the family and the reasons the family seems to require this role.
5. Plan a metacommunicative strategy designed to help the patient confront the problem with his or her family and interrupt dysfunctional behavioral sequences.
6. Implement the strategy and obtain feedback about its effectiveness.

In my clinical experience, once the patient has stopped or altered the behavior of the family members that reinforces dysfunctional patterns, the patient is usually freed to try out new and healthier role behaviors. Many can even do so without further assistance from the therapist. If the patient still has difficulty trying out new patterns due to paralyzing anxiety, more generic cognitive-behavioral techniques can then be used very effectively to push the patient forward. Such techniques become more effective than they would have been previously because the patient's family, if therapy has gone well, is no longer subverting the goals of therapy through the disqualification and invalidation of behavior change.

Before going further, I address two objections I have frequently heard to my recommendation that patients initiate metacommunication with dysfunctional parental figures.

TREATMENT RECOMMENDATIONS: CONTROVERSIES

Earlier, I discussed how looking at the contribution of a victimized patient to a dysfunctional interaction might incorrectly be characterized as "blaming the victim." The opposite contention is also made: Is unified therapy not engaging in parent bashing? Is it not providing the patient with a convenient scapegoat for his or her problems, and absolving them of all personal responsibility for their own misbehavior? Is it "letting the patient off the hook?"

Nothing is further from the truth. The unified therapist focuses on the responsibility of *both* the patient and the parents in dysfunctional interactions. I discussed earlier how adults past a certain age have at some point in their lives made a *decision* to act in dysfunctional ways, albeit out of altruistic intentions. The unified therapist has great empathy for the decision to act out a family script, but does not condone it. Although a therapist may or may not find the patient's behavior objectionable on moral grounds, the therapist does not dwell on morality. The therapist's main objection to the patient is a practical one: The behavior does not work for the purpose for which it was intended. It does not accomplish the goals it sets for itself. The patient is suffering in vain.

As we shall see, in unified therapy it is the patient who must alter his or her behavior before anyone else in the family does. This is framed as being necessary for the purpose of altering dysfunctional interactions in which all persons involved are playing a significant role. Nonetheless, it is the patient who must change first.

An important component of this change is the patient's development of empathy for the parents' conflicts. In unified therapy, it is important for the therapist to avoid portraying the parents as unredeemable villains, no matter how heinous their behavior. Helping the patient learn to be empathic with the parents without condoning bad behavior is one of the therapist's most important and difficult tasks. Such empathy is a prerequisite to successful metacommunication. A useful approach to teach the patient is to presume that everyone involved is trying to do the best they can (Hoffman, Fruzzetti, & Swenson, 1999).

Empathy does not mean the same as sympathy: The patient does not condone abusive parental behavior, but merely tries to understand it. To condone abusiveness is in fact unempathic because the parents know at some level that they have done wrong. If the patient were to say to them "it's OK that you did that," the parents would know immediately that the statement was insincere. The parents would know this because they are not stupid; they know abusing children is not OK. Furthermore, if it were all right, why would the patient be bringing it up as a problem to be solved?

Convincing patients to even consider developing empathy for abusive parents is difficult indeed. However, as Boszormenyi-Nagy and Krasner (1986) asked, if your parent is a monster and is a major contributor to who you are as a person, what does that make you? The job of therapy is not to punish wrongdoing but to solve problems that create wrongdoing.

A second major objection to the unified therapy paradigm that I often hear is that the risks to the patient of attempting to discuss family patterns with invalidating parents is too high. The parents are potentially violent in many instances. A patient's attempt to initiate such a discussion could ignite escalation of the invalidation and violence. A patient may try to do what the therapist assigns and have a disastrous result. They may come back to therapy in an emotional heap, if they come back at all. Furthermore, the fear of these potentially disastrous outcomes may motivate an alarmed spouse to "subvert" the intentions of the therapist, for fear that the spouse will be left alone to pick up the pieces.

Such risks are real. However, so are the risks inherent in not attempting to solve the problem. Invalidation with or without violence is an ongoing affair in these families. It could conceivably get even worse than it already is, but in most cases, it is already almost as bad as it possibly could be. I believe that the risks in making active interventions are worth taking; they are far surpassed by the benefits of a successful resolution.

More important, negative reactions are usually predictable and preventable. It is not so much a question of *whether* to confront these issues, but *how* they are confronted. In the chapter on role playing, we see how the therapist can anticipate the exact nature of problematic parental reactions and plan specific detailed strategies for preventing them. We also see how spouses can be kept informed of developments in the patient's therapy and become part of the solution rather than part of the problem. These strategies need to be tailor made to the particular family; generic "assertiveness" skills are often useless. In situations where the risk of family violence is high, family discussions can be held from a distance using the telephone.

Any treatment that has an active effect also has the potential to cause significant harm. The danger that a therapist might inadvertently increase the risk of a patient's suicide through his or her interventions is a constant presence in all psychotherapies. Therapists may forget about certain important factors when making homework assignments. Patients may behave in unpredictable ways or neglect to inform the therapist of essential information.

A particularly dramatic example of an unfortunate turn of events involved a client who had been a victim of extreme physical and sexual abuse as a child by both parents, but who nonetheless as an adult continued to visit them frequently. Her father, in fact, continued to strike her, although she was in her late 30s and bigger and stronger than he was. As is so often the case, the family had a strong taboo about discussing any of the abuse, despite the fact that it had always occurred openly. The patient, through lengthy therapy, gradually began to describe some of it to me. I, of course, responded with empathy to the new information and to her new openness.

I gave her specific instructions not to discuss the subject of the abuse with her parents until we had developed a strategy for doing so in which she would be safe and in which her parents were least likely to attack her or withdraw from her. Despite my warning, she became eager to break the family taboo and proceeded to do so. She brought up the childhood abuse to her mother; the mother responded by dragging the patient to the attic where most of the abuse had occurred. She took the patient to various spots where particularly horrendous activities had occurred and each time screamed to the patient, "Here's where [such and such] did *not* happen!" Naturally, the patient was terrified, and questioned the wisdom of continuing in therapy.

An interesting sidelight to the anecdote just mentioned is that the mother of the patient, in denying that the abuse took place, described in detail incidents of abuse without using any information volunteered by the patient. In the act of denying the abuse, she was admitting to it! Sometimes, even bad outcomes can eventually be turned to therapeutic advantage.

Family resistances to metacommunication are formidable; the heart of the therapy is finding ways to get past the obstacles family members throw up to avoid realistic discussions of conflictual issues. Denial is usually a big part of these family defenses, but it is well known and predictable. In fact, as pointed out by Barrett and Trepper (1992), families have multiple layers of denial that often come out in the same order. As one breaks through each of these resistances, the next one pops up in its place. The presence of denial is not a reason to avoid attempting to metacommunicate. The presence of multiple resistances represents multiple problems to be solved, not reasons for giving up.

Barrett and Trepper's predictable stages of denial are as follows:

1. Denial of facts ("it never happened; you're a liar!"), followed by:
2. Denial of awareness ("I was drunk," or "I didn't realize I was neglecting you; you should have told me"), followed by:
3. Denial of responsibility ("You were the one who was seductive," or "If your mother didn't deny me, I wouldn't have to have turned to you.") and finally:
4. Denial of impact ("It only happened a few times," or "It was *only* fondling," or "OK, so I beat you. Why do you always have to dwell on the past? You're just too sensitive; get over it!").

Barrett and Trepper, in the same article, said that they "... believe that some part of every offender is appalled by his own deeds and desperately yearns for the kind of inner peace and satisfaction found in healthy relationships not based on power, manipulation, and secrecy" (p. 41). As I discussed earlier, I concur wholeheartedly, although many therapists disagree.

Many versions of the "it's too risky" objection are based on an underlying premise that the patient is too "fragile" to engage in the process or that the family is too "disturbed" for a constructive outcome to transpire. I do not find either of these characterizations accurate in the vast majority of cases. Patients with BPD have often withstood unimaginable horrors; they are much stronger than we give them credit for. As to the families, they too are strong. We teach our patients not to be overprotective. Along with empathy, refusing to protect others from their bad feelings is a cornerstone of successful metacommunication. The importance of avoiding the "protection racket" is predicated on the idea that treating others as weak or impaired feeds into their feelings that they are weak and impaired. Treating them as strong and reasonable often leads them to behave in a strong and reasonable fashion. Therapists should be advised that this also holds true for patients with BPD as well as their family members.

The idea of treating BPD patients as if they are strong and reasonable is the basis of many interventions that have proved useful in getting them to stop acting out with the therapist, so that effective therapy can take place. In fact, therapists who successfully treat borderlines from a variety of psychotherapy schools use many of the same interventions for this purpose (Allen, 1997). This leads us to a discussion of the unified therapy conceptualization of transference and the methods by which transference acting out within the context of the therapeutic relationship is reduced. Transference is the subject of the next chapter.

6

Transference

Transference can be conceptualized as the enactment of role-relationship cognitive schemata or a script within the relationship between a patient and a psychotherapist. Patients bring schema-based relationship patterns to therapy. Because their script provides patients with a sense of existential meaning, patients will cling to them tenaciously. This is true even when their behavior is also making them completely miserable in every other conceivable way. It is no surprise that, even when coming to a therapist for help in changing maladaptive behavior, the patient will at first try to enlist the therapist as a source of support for the very behavior the patient is trying to alter.

Psychoanalytic writers discuss the concept of *projective identification*, an interpersonal dynamic in which a patient induces other people to serve as witting or unwitting accomplices in his or her dysfunctional behavior. If the patient is successful in this induction process, these other people then further reinforce, in the learning theory sense, his or her problematic behavior. For this reason, the schemata on which the behavior is based seem to be self-reinforcing. Therapists, of course, are prime targets for the BPD patient's projective identification.

Dysfunctional schemata or scripts are notoriously difficult to change in traditional therapies. This has led to the idea in some quarters that the schemata are so ingrained that they are unrespon-

*Portions of this chapter previously appeared in Allen, 1997.

sive to new information. The patient is seen as reacting to his or her environment according to his or her own preconceived ideas about how other people behave no matter how often these ideas are disconfirmed. I believe that such a conceptualization presupposes that human beings are amazingly stupid. I believe that schemata, although often enacted automatically and habitually in familiar appearing social situations, are amenable to change by ongoing current experience.

Many theorists have incompletely understood the cyclical process by which schemata are seemingly self-reinforced in repetitive interactions. Rather than patients being caught in an out-of-control feedback loop or a vicious circle, I have argued here and elsewhere (1988, 1991, 1993, 2001) that individuals are purposefully, and in a highly goal-directed manner, playing out roles that are highly valued by the their family of origin. However, despite this need for homeostasis within the family, schemata are in fact continuously updated by the Piagetian processes of assimilation and accommodation.

Although patients with personality disorders such as BPD in fact do respond to others according to their preformed expectations, I believe they only do so initially. The answer to the question of whether any preconceptions they may have are then altered depends on the result of a *series* of maneuvers and responses played out between the individuals in the relationship. If any individual's preformed expectations are not met, he or she—particularly if a personality disorder is present—will then actively work to *induce* others to respond according to those expectations. The fact that individuals can successfully induce another person to behave in certain ways creates the *illusion* that their internalized relationship scenarios are immutable and unresponsive to new information. If the induction is successful, others will eventually react precisely as the patient's schemata predict. In this sense, there is no "new" information to which the patient need accommodate.

However, I have found that, when consistently *unsuccessful* in provoking this outcome, people with personality disorders then can and do quickly alter both their behavior and their expectations. A caveat is that this relationship change occurs only in the relationship with the person who resists the induction—should that relationship even be allowed to continue. Other relationships—the ones outside of the relationship with the therapist in the case of a therapy relationship—go on much as before.

A patient comes to therapy secretly hoping that the therapist will act differently than his or her family, but expects to be treated in much the same way. If the therapist can not be induced to behave in the expected way despite the patient's best efforts to get them to do so—and patients are experts at getting others to do so—then the patient will usually settle down and behave in a reasonable fashion with the therapist. Although it may be difficult for many therapists to believe in light of their experience with the persistence of frustrating and annoying behavior from clients with BPD, this result can often be achieved relatively quickly. Therapists from a variety of schools who extensively deal with such patients have come to see this as true (Allen, 1997), although they may not conceptualize the process in quite the manner I have outlined.

Psychoanalytic treatments in the past have been predicated on the induction of a "transference neurosis." Analysts want the patient to focus their attention on the transference relationship with the therapist. This goal of analysis is based on the assumption that therapists will thereby gain some leverage in their here-and-now relationship with the patient. For this reason, almost everything the traditional analysand does is interpreted as a reaction to therapy, thereby hastening the development of a transference neurosis.

Unfortunately, this procedure created a problem for the analytic treatment of patients with BPD because the acting out of transference by these patients led to behavior that interfered with the very process of therapy itself. Spoiling behavior took place not merely in the form of devaluation of therapy and the therapist but in suicide threats and gestures, frantic late-night telephone calls, interference with the therapist's private life, or even interference with the therapist's treatment of other patients. For this reason, analysts used to label patients with BPD "un-analyzable." Analytic techniques had to be significantly modified by innovators such as Otto Kernberg and James Masterson in order to treat these patients with a psychodynamic approach.

Unified therapy attempts to "eliminate the middle man." The healing powers of the relationship between the patient and the therapist are thought to be no match for the homeostatic—and mutative—powers of the patient's current and ongoing interactions with his or her family of origin. The unified therapist wants the patient in therapy to focus on the family patterns outside of therapy in a way that is as reasoned and objective as possible, so that the therapist can plan strategies for altering them. The therapist does, however, look at transference patterns; they are seen as a source of information about the family patterns because, after all, they are a reenactment of those patterns. However, "cures" based on analysis of the transference are believed to be quickly overcome by ongoing family relationships outside of therapy. Changes in the relationship with the therapist do not generalize to important relationships outside of therapy because the patient's outside behavior is met with reactions that are not at all similar to those of the therapist. For this reason, transference is not the major focus of unified therapy.

The therapist certainly can not ignore transference acting out. In fact, the therapist must be alert to potential transference reactions because, as mentioned, they often serve as resistances and impede therapy. The therapist should consistently attempt to change the focus of the client from the therapist back on to a discussion of family dynamics.

The overall strategy for doing so is the avoidance of interventions or attitudes that are pathologizing, that is, those that assume that the patient's reactions to the therapist occur because the patient is overly dependent, unreasonable, cognitively impaired, immature, foolish, or stupid. The therapist should not belabor the obvious, instruct the patient on the obvious drawbacks to certain courses of action, or imply that the patient's reactions are not mature or justified. The therapist may point out that patient's reactions might seem to be unjustified, but that the therapist suspects otherwise. All interventions mentioned in the following discussion should be made in a matter-of-fact, friendly, nondefensive way.

The following are some of the types of patient behavior to which the therapist should respond using the transference-reducing interventions that are described in more detail shortly:

1. Significant acting-out behavior that directly involves the therapist.
2. Seemingly inappropriate or exaggerated responses to requests or interpretations from the therapist.
3. Metaphorical concerns about the nature of the therapeutic relationship.

4. Disqualification or invalidation of the therapist.
5. Self-denigrating explanations for maladaptive behavior that are meant to encourage a negative judgment from the therapist.

As mentioned, patients with BPD are believed to have an expectancy that the therapist will react to their provocations in much the same way as their families often do. They will habitually, and without much thought, engage in their typical behavior, thereby giving the therapist the opportunity and justification for doing so. On the other hand, they desperately hope that the therapist will act differently than their families. Although attempting to induce the therapist to recreate aspects of their family environment, patients with BPD are actually highly ambivalent about doing so.

This model predicts that any time the patient successfully recreates maladaptive aspects of his or her family environment in the relationship with the therapist, the likelihood of additional provocative behavior increases, whereas any time the patient is unable to do so the likelihood decreases. The therapist uses knowledge of this process, knowledge of the patient and his or her social and family history, observations of transference reactions, an understanding of typical family characteristics of patients with BPD, and the feelings that the patient induces in him or her to shape a corrective response pattern.

As a backdrop for understanding interventions that decrease acting out by BPD patients with a therapist, let us first examine the possible reactions a naïve helping professional might have in response to troublesome BPD behavior. The provocative behavior of the patient with BPD would seem naturally to induce a certain range of reactions from others within the social context of a relationship between a concerned caretaker and the person cared for. That is, in contexts similar to psychotherapy, an average person would react to BPD behavior in predictable ways that, according to the theory, parallel the previously described negative reactions by family members to patients with the disorder. The caretaker's own predispositions and conflicts would determine the particular reaction from within that spectrum of likely possibilities that he or she actually would exhibit.

Almost any caretaker, when persistently confronted by the troublesome acting-out behavior characteristic of the patient with BPD in therapy, would naturally begin to feel any or all of the following:

angry, used, abused, unappreciated, unreasonably attacked, disempowered, guilty about not being able to relieve the patient's suffering, or anxious about the ramifications of the patient's symptoms. Anxiety caused by a sense of guilt, inadequacy, helplessness, or frustration might lead caretakers to search for ways to make a patient feel better quickly, even in the face of help-rejecting responses by the patient. Alternatively, the caretaker might reluctantly indulge the patient's unreasonable demands, either out of a sense of pity, a wish to placate the patient, or a misguided hope of ridding themselves of the problem.

When such efforts fail, as they often do, patients with BPD usually become even more critical and negativistic toward a caretaker than they were initially. This sequence, in turn, has a high probability of leading a caretaker to become hostile. This hostility would in most instances be coupled with blame and criticism of the patient for the unreasonable behavior. The hostility might be overt in the form of mean-spirited personal attacks or subtle in the form of pejorative interpretations or infantalizing attributions to or about the patient. Alternatively, the patient might be accused of being unaware of the damage he or she is causing—a subtle accusation of lack of intelligence—through the use of pointing out the obvious or lecturing the patient. Last, the patient might be abruptly abandoned altogether. These reactions recreate the family environment of the patient with BPD.

All of the therapeutic techniques to be discussed in this chapter may be conceptualized as ways to prevent therapists from falling into the trap of behaving in the just-mentioned manner. These interventions seem to alter this entire sequence of events and help the therapist to avoid hostility, anxiety, and guilt. Therapists instead present themselves as comfortable with their own limitations and unwilling to make unusual or risky interventions; unafraid of the patient's anger, neediness, or anxiety; and unwilling to attack the patient in the face of provocation. They do not rush in to "take care" of the patient in an infantalizing manner. They are in tune with and respectful of their own needs.

Therapists are relentlessly respectful of the patient's suffering, abilities, and values. They communicate an expectation that the patient will be able to behave in a reasonable and cooperative manner, and they play to the patients' strengths. They presume that patients with BPD have the wherewithal to go through the anxiety-pro-voking process of therapy like any other patient. Finally, the technique employed to handle any therapist errors may interrupt the process by which problematic behaviors are reinforced on a variable intermittent reinforcement schedule by the therapist's mistakes.

The recommended approach seems to have a calming effect on patients with BPD in many instances. Patients tend to become less difficult, less crisis-oriented, and more cooperative. They tend to start working harder on those areas in their lives that can be changed through the process of therapy.

We discuss shortly several useful therapist interventions that help decrease transference reactions and resistances. These interventions include using the treatment contracting process, making paradoxical predictions, discounting "obvious" explanations for the patient's behavior, using disclaimers, employing specific countermeasures for each type of disqualifying or provocative behavior, and looking for reasonable motives behind dysfunctional behavior. Naturally, none of these interventions works all the time, and therapists may need to try out several different ones on a given patient before achieving the desired results.

Before discussing these specific interventions, let us first look at how the unified therapist handles some of the so-called "parameters" of treatment (Eissler, 1953) that psychoanalysts discuss whenever they talk about trying to *create* a transference neurosis. In unified therapy, they are handled somewhat differently than in psychoanalysis, so that transference reactions are reduced rather than reinforced.

PARAMETERS OF TREATMENT

1. Personal questions: Therapists should quickly and honestly answer brief questions about themselves that are not particularly personal, loaded, wide-ranging, or intrusive, but respond to loaded or extensive personal questions with, "We're here to talk about you, not me."
2. Gifts: Therapists may accept small gifts at Christmas with thanks and without additional comment, but refuse gifts that are large or inappropriately timed. In the latter case, the therapist expresses concern that the gift may have some unclear

meaning that might affect therapy—without insisting that this must be true.

3. Reactions to events in therapy: Therapists should assume that the patient's reactions to events in therapy are sensible and appropriate unless there is significant, clear evidence to the contrary. For instance, if the therapist is late for a session or makes a mistake in scheduling, he or she should apologize but should not make inquiries into the patient's reactions about the error *unless* the patient continues to focus, directly or in metaphor, on the event. If the patient is, on rare occasions, late for a session, the therapist may inquire as to the reason but should generally assume that the tardiness is not worthy of extensive exploration, even if the patient indicates that the reason is that the patient is somewhat uncomfortable with the material from the last session. If, on the other hand, there is a pattern of lateness, or if the therapist has reason to believe that the patient may be thinking seriously about quitting therapy, more extensive exploration of the patient's behavior is in order. The therapist should then begin with the assumption that the patient has some underlying concerns about therapy that have not been expressed. Once again, however, the therapist should assume that those concerns are reasonable.

4. Therapist vacations: If the therapist is about to go on a vacation of more than a week, he or she might make a paradoxical prediction (see "paradoxical predictions" to follow) such as "Sometimes when therapy is interrupted, patients have a natural tendency, because therapy is often uncomfortable, to want to stop coming. I hope that won't happen with you." The therapist should then drop the issue. This intervention is generally made only the first time a therapist takes a vacation during a given patient's therapy.

5. Unusual but short-lived reactions to the therapist: Ignoring transference reactions of short duration may at times be an effective intervention. Doing so might be appropriate in cases in which a patient who has previously been in dynamic or experiential therapy makes a statement clearly designed to induce the therapist to focus on the transference. The therapist might also ignore a comment with possibly insulting implications about the therapist if the patient then abruptly drops the issue.

TREATMENT CONTRACTING

Yeomans, Selzer, and Clarkin (1992) outlined a procedure for setting a treatment contract with patients with BPD who undergo the psychoanalytic treatment paradigm developed by Kernberg. Preliminary studies have shown that if the therapist sets up the contract properly, patients with BPD are often able to follow its terms much of the time. Of course, some testing by the patient of the therapist's resolve to stick to the terms of the contract is inevitable, but it is often easily stopped. The use of contracting also seems to reduce the rate of attrition from therapy.

The contracting procedure centers on explaining to the patient that, in order for therapy to work, certain basic conditions for therapy must be met. These basic conditions are then specified to the patient and are presented as nonnegotiable. Patient behaviors that will interfere with the process of therapy are explicitly characterized to the patient as such.

The therapist does not begin treatment unless the patient agrees to the terms of the contract. The therapist refuses to be drawn into arguments with patients about whether or not they have the ability to stick to the terms of the proposed contract; if they do not or will not or can not, Kernberg's form of therapy is presented as simply not possible. Should this be the case, the patient is advised to seek an alternate form of treatment from another therapist skilled in a different type of therapy. The therapist presents the contract in a matter-of-fact, nonjudgmental way and describes its terms as deriving from the requirements of the therapy method, not from the idiosyncratic needs of the therapist per se.

Some of the terms to which the patient must agree are coming regularly and on time, maintaining financial support so as to be able to continue to afford treatment, staying for the entire session, and speaking freely about all subjects. The patient is not to expect the therapist to engage in activities that are labeled *case management* such as giving advice, arranging for social services, or being available for chronic crisis management.

Patient behaviors that have caused difficulties in a particular patient's previous therapy experience, such as excessive intrusions into the therapist's private life, are identified. The therapist then expresses his or her concerns about how these behaviors may interfere with treatment again and invites the patient to participate in a plan to safeguard therapy. If patients break terms of the contract later in therapy, they are tactfully questioned about why they are attempting to subvert their therapy.

Therapists who employ Linehan's (1993) dialectical behavior therapy present a treatment contract to patients in much the same way as Kernberg's group, with only somewhat different contract terms. They too label certain troublesome behaviors as "therapy interfering." The terms of both Kernberg's and Linehan's treatment contracts seem to require a degree of impulse control on the part of the patient of which some therapists believe patients with BPD incapable. In Kernberg's therapy, for instance, if patients feel that they are about to harm themselves, they are instructed not to call the therapist but to go to an emergency room and follow whatever recommendations are given to them there. They are told that the therapist will not manage their care when they are hospitalized because of the nature of Kernberg's treatment. If it is true that many patients with BPD can for the most part keep to the terms of such treatment contracts, it may be that they have considerably more impulse control than conventional wisdom suggests.

As is discussed in detail in the next chapter, unified therapists offer patients an initial explanation of how therapy will proceed that functions much like a treatment contract. They explicitly ask the patient for agreement in following the plan. If and when difficulties arise, the patient is quickly informed about which behaviors will increase the likelihood that the therapy will be successful, and which will decrease it. In most cases, it is then left up to patients to decide whether or not they want therapy to work. If the therapist is asked to do something that will actively interfere with the likelihood of successful therapy, he or she politely refuses to do so. Explanations for such refusals are kept to a minimum; the therapist presumes that the patient in reality already knows why the therapist is refusing because the reasons are usually obvious (see "refusing to argue" in the section on countering disqualifications further on in this chapter).

PARADOXICAL PREDICTIONS

Early in the process of therapy, often during the initial evaluation, patients will almost invariably telegraph to the therapist how their relationships usually turn out, and imply or state that these relationships have been disappointing or problematic. The therapist can then anticipate that the patient probably will at some point in therapy behave in ways designed to create within the therapeutic relationship the very outcome the patient is complaining about, and for which the therapist will be criticized.

Therapists can subtly head off the tendency of BPD patients to elicit these feared negative reactions through the use of interventions called *paradoxical predictions*. Therapists should be on the lookout for opportunities to make paradoxical predictions in the first two to three sessions. The therapist predicts that, because patients have had the same type of negative experiences and reactions so repeatedly from others, there may come a time when the patient gets the feeling that the therapist is acting in a similar manner. Should this occur, the therapist continues, it is important that the patient bring it up for discussion, so the therapist can address the issue with the patient. This way, any misunderstandings can be cleared up. For example, one patient complained that no one in her family took her opinions seriously, although she considered herself to be quite knowledgeable. The therapist told her that, because of this experience, there might come a time when she would feel that he was not taking her opinions seriously.

Paradoxical predictions are paradoxical because they tend to decrease the likelihood that the predicted occurrence will actually come to pass. The acknowledgment by the therapist of the issue and his or her bold offer to talk about it should it happen is a refreshing departure from the patient's usual experience. In many instances, the patient's family members have refused, through whatever means necessary, to validate the patient's perceptions about the problem. They may have even denied that the problem exists. This immediate difference between the reactions of the patient's family and the therapist often allows patients to bypass some of the usual testing of the therapist. Patients feel less need to check to see if the therapist is really going to be different from everybody else. Because a "testing" phase can take up a great many therapy sessions, reducing it shortens therapy considerably.

The usual patient response to the paradoxical prediction is something like, "Oh, I don't think that you're like that" or "I'm determined that I'm not going to react that way this time." The therapist then replies, "OK, but let's keep an eye out for it." He or she then completely drops the subject.

Paradoxical predictions should be used sparingly by the therapist. Usually, the therapist should make only one or two. Paradoxical predictions should never be repeated. If the therapist keeps bringing up a problem that has not yet arisen, patients may infer from the therapist's preoccupation with it that the therapist will be disappointed if it does *not* arise. They may then go ahead and provide it.

If, despite the skillful application of the paradoxical prediction, the issue does arise later in therapy, the patient has contracted to discuss it. The therapist can then remind the patient that they had agreed to keep an eye out for the problem so that it might be resolved. In response, patients tend to drop the issue. If they do not, they have committed to discussing it. Either way, the problem usually gets resolved quickly.

DISCOUNTING "OBVIOUS" EXPLANATIONS FOR PATIENT MISBEHAVIOR

Alternately or in addition to telegraphing relationship issues, patients in the beginning of therapy may proudly exhibit a persona or false self that seems to invite a negative evaluation or criticism from the therapist. It may almost seem that the patient has read sections of the DSM, which describes personality disorders in rather pejorative language. For example, the DSM-IV describes a patient with narcissistic traits as "... interpersonally exploitative, i.e., takes advantage of others to achieve his or her own ends" and "lacks empathy: is unwilling to recognize or identify with the feelings and needs of others" (APA, 1994, p. 661).

Such a description glosses over the low self-esteem, desperation and frustration these patients have over the lack of appreciation they receive from others. Ostensibly, narcissistic patients may seem to want to control other individuals for some selfish intention, but they are often trying to take care of a help-rejecting loved one. They may have to cover this softer side of themselves up and act like bullies in order to give the loved one an excuse to continue his or her own help rejecting ways, or to prevent the other from becoming even more self-destructive than he or she already is.

Psychotherapy pioneer Karen Horney coined the term *neurotic pride* (Symonds & Symonds, 1985) to describe the phenomenon in which patients exhibiting a rather unattractive persona seem to take a perverse sort of pride in their negative image. In unified therapy, individuals who do so are thought to be purposely portraying themselves in a bad light in order to cover up their self-sacrificing behavior. This false self with its false pride is often very convincing to others—so much so that therapists often miss the hidden sacrifice.

Therapists can often help a patient stop using neurotic pride as a resistance to therapy by themselves acknowledging the negative persona and then discounting it. For example, the therapist might say to a patient who seems to meet the negative narcissistic stereotype: "Some people might think you act the way you do because you are all wrapped up in yourself and insensitive to others; I don't believe it; I can see how caring you are." As with paradoxical predictions, the therapist must make use of such comments sparingly and not repeat them. The goal of the intervention is not to "unmask" the patient or to make him or her give up a false self. A persona serves an important purpose for the patient and can not and should not be taken away before the reasons for its existence are identified and remedied. The goal of the intervention is rather to reduce the pressure that the patient feels to convince the therapist that he or she is as bad as he or she might seem on initial and casual inspection.

Patients often respond to this intervention with a look that seems to say "no comment." Rarely will patients argue that they really are as bad as they seem to be, although this does happen from time to time. If the patient does not respond, therapists should make no further comments about the issue. If instead an argument ensues, therapists should calmly state that they are merely reporting an impression that is open to change, and neither argue nor belabor the point. What seems to remain with patients after this sequence is completed is an unspoken sense that the therapist believes that they are basically good, without any pressure to immediately change their outward presentation. Paradoxically, their presentation in the relationship with the therapist usually softens.

DISCLAIMERS

In unified therapy, therapists have to bring up and explore a patient's problematic or counterproductive behavior, and describe potentially unflattering hypotheses about the patient's family relationship patterns. Patients have a natural tendency to become

defensive in these situations, and the therapist runs the risk of provoking a transference reaction of some sort. The use of a disclaimer
often makes the initiation of such discussions more palatable to the
patient. Disclaimers are pre-statements that acknowledge the potentially unpleasant nature of the issue at hand, proclaim the lack of
any ill intent on the part of the therapist, and give patients or their
family members the benefit of the doubt concerning their motivation for engaging in problematic behavior. Disclaimers can also be
used to avoid power struggles that tend to occur when the therapist
sounds like a know-it-all or like someone trying to "put one over"
on the patient.

The use of disclaimers by a therapist decreases the likelihood that
patients will get defensive and increases the likelihood that they will
consider the merits of the therapist's proposition. Later in unified
therapy, therapists teach patients to make use of disclaimers during
metacommunication with their family about relationship patterns
and issues. Disclaimers are just as effective in that context.

Disclaimers can be used in innumerable ways. A few examples
will be given here of types of clinical situations in which disclaimers
are useful. The examples are also meant to give the reader a general
idea about how disclaimers should be phrased.

1. The therapist must bring up a patient's seemingly provocative
   behavior. The therapist might say something such as, "I know
   you're not trying to anger me when you do that, but when you
   do [such and such], it would be easy for someone who did not
   know you so well to get the wrong idea."
2. Patients may hold an unexpressed belief that a family member is purposely "asking for" or trying to elicit a nasty response from them. They may be reluctant to say so, however,
   for fear the therapist will brand them as self-serving or even
   crazy. The therapist can often get the patient to acknowledge
   such thoughts by putting the burden of "craziness" on himself or herself: "This is probably going to sound crazy, but I
   wonder if sometimes you get the idea that your mother *wants*
   you to steal money from her. After all, she keeps leaving it in
   plain sight."
3. The therapist wants to bring up for discussion the obvious
   ways that the patient's behavior causes problems without

sounding like a critical parent or insulting the patient's intelligence. The therapist might say, "At risk of sounding just like your mother, and as I'm sure you already know, attacking your father does not seem to solve anything."

4. Patients often describe relationship patterns that superficially resemble patterns that the therapist has seen in many other families. The therapist may want to offer up for discussion a possible interpretation of this family behavior that the patient may not have considered. This may take place before the therapist has gathered enough evidence to make the case that the interpretation actually applies to the patient's family. Much time in therapy can be saved, should it turn out that the family behavior is explained by the typical interpretation, if the therapist does not have to wait until the patient happens to volunteer the necessary information. If it is not yet known whether the patient's family fits the hypothesis, the best way to find out is by offering the interpretation to the patient for consideration as a possible explanation of the problematic family interactions. Unfortunately, the patient may take umbrage at the implications of such a hypothesis. This happens for many reasons, including that the possibility that the interpretation in question is flat out wrong. Giving the patient an "out" so that he or she can easily reject the proposal without seeming to challenge the therapist can solve this problem. The therapist can say, "I don't know if this applies to your family or not, but in other families I've seen where this sort of thing happens, [such and such] leads to the behavior you describe. Do you think that this might apply to your situation?"

5. A therapist wants to bring up the behavior of family members who seem to be contributing to the patient's problems. In response, patients may often become defensive about their families. They do so despite the fact that they themselves are at wit's end with the relative seemingly under the therapist's attack. Defending one's family from outside attack even if one is angry at them is quite a natural reaction, but may preclude much useful discussion about the possible reasons for the family member's misbehavior. A useful disclaimer that may prevent this from happening is, "I'm not trying to turn you father into a villain, but ..."

COUNTERING INVALIDATION

The premise behind the interventions described in this section is that responses by the therapist that are indicative of rage, guilt, or anxious helplessness will likely increase, on a basis analogous to a variable intermittent reinforcement schedule, the frequency of the patient's spoiling responses in therapy. The therapist does not have to express such feelings overtly; they can be communicated in very subtle ways, such as lecturing a client or making "accusatory interpretations." Infantalizing the patient through lecturing is often a veiled form of hostility or defensiveness, as are many interpretations that imply that clients are unconsciously childish, immature, malevolent, stupid, insane, or inherently defective.

If the therapist can instead react to various provocations with increased concern, interest, understanding, and empathy—without any guilt or anxiety over the fact that the therapist is in no way able to meet unreasonable demands or provide a quick panacea—then the client will stop spoiling and get down to the work of therapy. This conceptualization creates a systematic framework for understanding some commonly used therapeutic countermoves to spoiling behavior, as well as for the innovation of some new ones.

A word of caution here: Because this formulation posits a paradigm analogous to a variable intermittent reinforcement schedule, the therapist will get into trouble if he or she even on rare occasions reacts with rage, guilt, or helplessness. Avoiding such responses can be a real challenge, because clients with BPD are experts at determining how best to elicit them. BPD patients will systematically alter their behavior until they find a way that is most likely to bring about negative countertransference from any particular person.

The following are some effective countermoves for the most typical borderline provocations. Suggestions for countering therapist errors are also presented so that the therapist can avoid falling into the trap of intermittently reinforcing spoiling responses. All of the suggested interventions should be made by the therapist using a pleasant, matter of fact, and nondefensive tone of voice.

1. The patient makes wild accusations or exaggerated overgeneralizations such as "You don't care about me; you're only in it for the money" or "Everyone will exploit you if given half a

chance; the world is nothing but a toilet bowl." The problem here is that if you agree with the patient, you are collaborating in the hyperbole as well as saying negative things about that denizen of the toilet bowl—yourself. On the other hand, if you tell patients in so many words that they do not know what they are talking about, then you are invalidating them and putting them down. Solution (courtesy of Rodney Burgoyne, [personal communication]): In this situation, one looks for the kernel of truth in the patient's statement, validates it, and completely ignores the hyperbole or accusation. To the first statement one might casually and nondefensively reply, "Well as you know this is the way I make my living." To the second, one might reply empathetically, "It sounds like you must have been really mistreated in your life."

2. A variation on this theme takes place when the client uses a nasty tone of voice to imply some misdeed on the part of the therapist, but the lexical content of the verbalization does not overtly make an accusation. Most people, including therapists, tend to react to the tone of voice instead of the words (Allen, 1991); if on the other hand the therapist responds only to the words, the client usually changes to a friendlier tone. For example, a client with panic disorder responded to a recommendation for antidepressant medication with the sarcastic-sounding remark, "Oh, so you want to mess with my brain chemistry?" It sounded as though she was accusing her therapist of being a devious, malicious mad scientist. He nonchalantly responded, "Yes, antidepressants do alter brain chemistry" and went on to describe their purported mechanism of action just as one might do with any other patient. She agreed to the drug trial.

3. The client demands premature therapist interventions or immediate and unattainable relief from unhappiness, or makes inappropriate and disruptive claims on the therapist's time. For example, the therapist may get an "emergency" telephone call at a strange hour because the patient is upset over something that happened earlier that day. The patient may demand that the therapist offer advice about how to handle the problem before the therapist even knows all the relevant parameters. Solution: Admit helplessness. In anticipation of this kind of behavior, the therapist's first words in response can be, "There's

probably not going to be much I can do to help you right now, but go ahead and tell me what's going on." Often this is enough to nip provocative behavior in the bud, but if the patient goes on to criticize one's ineptitude, one can reply, "Yeah, I feel really bad that I can't make this better for you quickly. I sure wish I knew the answer already." The advantage of these comments, which may seem to be paradoxical, is that they happen to be true. It is wise to assume that the patient already knows that the therapist can not be of much help in such a situation, but to avoid expressing anger at the patient for the intrusion.

Another useful response to inappropriate late-night telephone calls is an earnest, pleasant, and nonaccusatory, "Would you do me a favor and call back after 9 a.m.? I'd really appreciate it." I was pleasantly surprised the first few times I tried saying that to a patient; patients with BPD often readily agree to do so! They may even apologize: "Oh, I'm sorry, did I wake you?"

4. Patients make absurd arguments or patently irrational statements, such as arguing that they take dangerous drugs because drugs are really good for them. Solution: Respect the client's intelligence by politely refusing to argue. One can say, "I won't insult your intelligence by arguing with that," or "You've already told me how miserable the drugs have made your life; there must be a good reason why you continue to act in such a self-destructive manner." If clients go on to insist that they really do believe that dangerous drugs are good, the therapist can look for some way in which their self-destructive behavior does in fact solve some family problem. The drugs do make the client "feel better"—but only in that one special sense. Alternatively, one can state, "I do not agree with you," without going on to argue about who is right or wrong. Many clients with BPD have never experienced a respectful disagreement in their entire lives.

5. The patient makes vague suicide threats, usually accompanied by some form of oppositional or provocative behavior such as refusing to agree to a no-suicide contract. (The issue of self-mutilation as opposed to suicidality is discussed separately in the next chapter). In such instances, the patient is likely to be using talk about suicide to make the therapist feel helpless and anxious. Solution: Make a paradoxical offer to hospitalize the patient. Clients with BPD are notorious for acting out and getting

much worse in psychiatric hospitals. If at all avoidable, the hospital is the last place on earth they should be. A response that is often helpful in avoiding the need for hospitalization is, "If you really think you might kill yourself, then you need to be in the hospital, but only for your own protection. I'd really be concerned that you'd feel a lot worse about yourself there than you already do being thrown in with a bunch of crazy people."

Clients frequently respond to this intervention with something like, "I'll be alright, I guess" or words to that effect. Unfortunately, these words are often said using a rather nonreassuring tone of voice that makes the statement sound questionable. In such cases, I respond to the lexical content as described earlier, and tell the patient I will see them at their next regularly scheduled visit.

When patients respond to the intervention with, "I am *going* to kill myself unless you put me in the hospital," I will usually comply, albeit reluctantly. However, because the therapist has told the patient that the hospitalization probably will not help, the paradoxical offer often sets up a scenario in which the hospitalization is brief. When a hospitalized patient asks to be discharged, I almost invariably comply.

Occasionally, I have gone to much trouble to arrange for hospitalization only to find out the next day that the patients did not go. When I call to find out what happened, they tell me that they changed their minds because they started to feel a little better. The therapist's gut reaction in this case is likely to be anger at the patient because of all the time and trouble spent by the therapist getting pre-authorization from the patient's insurance company, calling with admitting orders, and so forth. Therapists should remind themselves that the outcome in this situation—no hospitalization—is the one they had preferred in the first place.

The paradoxical offer to hospitalize need not be used if the patient merely says, "I'm *thinking* about suicide" as opposed to "I am *going* to kill myself." The patient with BPD thinks about suicide much of the time. The former statement is merely one meant to communicate that the patient is in distress about something, mixed in with the usual "hook" that invites the therapist to over-react.

Novice therapists should err on the side of hospitalization more than experienced therapists because the former have less experience in determining which suicide threats are serious and which probably are not. Protecting oneself against potential legal liability problems should always be an important consideration for a therapist. Whenever patients force the therapist's hand, the therapist should put them in the hospital. Having said that, however, therapists should remind themselves that a patient who is highly intent on suicide can not really be stopped no matter what the therapist does. Currently there is no evidence that hospitalizing patients with BPD has any effect on suicide rates whatsoever.

If patients call with a serious suicide threat but refuse to disclose their whereabouts or state they will just leave if the therapist calls 911, the therapist is truly powerless. I have found that the best reply is "I sure hope you don't do it." If the patient then answers back with, "You don't really care," the therapist can reply, "I wish there was some way I could convince you that I do."

6. The client makes a damaging or incendiary accusation about an important referral source, or about a colleague who is well respected or who is even a friend of the therapist. This is a variant on the infamous "staff split" in hospital situations in which the client gets various people to fight with one another. In transactional analysis terms, it is a game of "let's you and him fight." If therapists defend the accused without having an impartial account of what actually transpired, they are invalidating the patient. However, the patient may be exaggerating what happened, making undue inferences about the motives of the accused, or discounting the role of his or her own provocative behavior in the dispute. Solution: State, "I was not there, and I have a different impression of him from my other contacts, so I am not in a position to make a judgment on this." The therapist then refuses to take either side.

One major exception to this recommendation is when a patient alleges that a former therapist had a sexual relationship with the patient. Such an allegation should be taken very seriously because, in my experience, patients rarely make unfounded allegations about this subject. With the patient's agreement, appropriate legal steps can be recommended. The therapist must keep in mind that patients with BPD often make poor witnesses, so the possible deleterious effect on the patient of taking action needs to be considered. However, the therapist can help the patient to be a better witness if necessary.

7. No matter what the therapist says, the client escalates with more and more outrageous accusations or oppositionalism. Solution: Inquire, "Why are you picking a fight with me?" Once again, the therapist refuses to argue the obvious by debating whether or not the client is indeed picking a fight. This intervention seems to impel the client to either stop the behavior and go on to some other subject, or to stop the behavior in order to explore it. However, it is only effective after many other interventions have been tried but have failed to calm the transference storm. The reason for this is, in order for the therapist to be confident that the patient truly is picking a fight, the patient's negative patient behavior must have already persisted in the face of consistent efforts by the therapist to be conciliatory.

8. The patient suddenly drops transference acting out right in the middle of a heated interaction and instead begins to describe his or her family interactions. For example, a client may seemingly be in a rage over some imagined slight attributed to the therapist, but then abruptly calm down and begin to talk about family members as if the feelings about the therapist had never come up. In analytically oriented therapies, where transference is central, the usual response by the therapist in this situation is to bring the discussion back to the transference reaction. However, because the goal of the unified therapist is to reduce transference resistances and find out why the patient is acting in such a way in first place, then the therapist should also stop discussing the transference battle and let the patient go on with the discussion of the family situation. The therapist should not bring up the dispute again unless the patient does.

Because of the abrupt nature of the change in subject, the therapist may feel drawn back to the transference issue. This happens because the interaction that preceded the switch feels unfinished. The feeling is somewhat akin to the way one feels when one has repeatedly tried to get a loquacious friend off the telephone after a protracted conversation, and the friend angrily says, "OK, good-bye!" The natural response is "No, wait!" although ending the conversation had been one's goal in the first place. The therapist should resist the temptation to re-ignite the transference battle.

9. The patient gets the best of the therapist and the therapist reacts with a statement or action that invalidates or insults the patient. Despite being well versed in the kinds of interventions described in this section, the therapist may still find himself or herself responding poorly to the patient's provocations. The patient, after all, has a lifetime of experience in creating these reactions, and the therapist is a relative newcomer to the process. Unfortunately, intermittent emotional overreactions from the therapist will lead the client to try even harder and longer to induce the therapist to overreact again. Solution:

   A. Be good-natured about your error. After all, you are only human. Be able to laugh at yourself. Say, "Gee, I sure did get frustrated with you that time."

   B. Apologize for your error, but not for the feelings that led to it. Example: "I am sorry for sounding so critical, but I just had the feeling that you were dismissing everything I said out of hand."

LOOKING FOR REASONABLE MOTIVES FOR DYSFUNCTIONAL BEHAVIOR

The unified therapist should consistently maintain to patients that their apparently dysfunctional behavior must have some understandable and reasonable motive behind it; they are not acting in a problematic way because they are inherently crazy, immature, cognitively impaired, malevolent, masochistic, or mentally retarded. Therapists should maintain this positive regard for the patient's motives and intelligence without necessarily condoning any particular behavior. The therapist refuses to agree with any comments that patients make about themselves that employ or imply any of the previously listed explanations for their own behavior.

When the patient first describes self-destructive behavior, the therapist makes the following type of intervention: "You certainly must have a good reason for doing that to yourself; you are certainly not enjoying yourself and I don't believe in masochism." For a patient stuck in an abusive relationship, the therapist can remark, "You certainly must care a lot about that person or you wouldn't put up with that." When patients entirely blame themselves for any sort of interpersonal problem, the therapist might say, "That's very kind of you to put all the blame on yourself."

Most of the interventions described in this chapter are primarily used in the first few sessions of therapy, but they can be used at any time throughout the entire therapy course. They are particularly useful in reducing the patient's resistances to candidly providing information that will clarify the psychosocial variables that trigger and reinforce the patient's dysfunctional behavior. In the next chapter, we look in detail at how to use the initial evaluation of patients with BPD in ways that also help achieve this goal in a timely fashion.

7

Initial Evaluation

In the process of initiating unified therapy, issues of diagnosis, symptomatic treatment, and the setting up of the initial treatment contract are addressed in the first two to three visits. I find that the medical model for history taking works well as an initial strategy with patients with BPD. Despite the concerns of some clinicians, the medical model does not preclude the clinician from eventually moving from directive questioning toward collaborative exploration. Nor must it lead to a dehumanizing or mechanical approach to the patient. Although making a diagnosis on a patient may, as some have suggested, lead to a lack of further critical thinking by a therapist, it does not have to do so. It can instead be used for the purpose of finding effective treatments for psychiatric symptoms exhibited by the particular patient that, if not remedied, would impede the process of therapy.

In addition to diagnosing comorbid conditions that might respond to symptomatic treatment, the medical model of history taking allows the therapist to obtain a lot of useful information early in therapy that patients might not otherwise reveal. Under the guise of leaving no stone unturned, the therapist can probe the most sensitive areas of the patient's life without implying that these areas are necessarily contributing to the patient's distress. This manner of questioning leads patients to feel less need to defend themselves or their families. On occasion I have been told about important historical information during an initial interview that patients later deny. A relatively complete history helps the therapist to more quickly understand the meaning behind much of what the patient says as therapy progresses.

USE OF MEDICATION

The use of medications or other forms of symptomatic treatment is encouraged in unified therapy. Psychiatric medications often help the process of therapy because debilitating psychiatric symptoms are usually stirred up or exacerbated by focused discussions about the psychosocial processes that trigger them in the first place. The presence of such symptoms makes it more difficult for patients to continue in therapy, maintain their focus and concentration, or do homework assignments. In other words, psychiatric symptoms interfere with the process of therapy itself. In particular, patients with BPD tend to be emotionally hyperreactive with therapists and therapy. By necessity, however, therapists must forthrightly delve into the patient's most sensitive issues.

As of this writing no medication exists that can directly alter specific dysfunctional interpersonal behavior patterns. The only exception to this rule is the rare patient with an affective or anxiety disorder who has significant borderline traits during an episode that completely disappear once the Axis I disorder is treated with antidepressant medication. I believe it highly unlikely that psychotherapy will ever become unnecessary for the treatment of true personality disorders due to the development of new medications. For this reason, psychotherapy remains the most important part of treatment. However, for quick relief of symptoms, medication usually beats psychotherapy hands down.

For nonmedical therapists, it is important to find a prescribing psychiatrist with whom to collaborate who will not interfere with the process of psychotherapy. Finding such a physician may be difficult, but well worth the effort. Psychiatrists or other physicians unfamiliar with the treatment paradigm should be educated about it. In particular, the rationale for controversial treatment decisions such as refusing to hospitalize a patient threatening suicide should be explained to them, and their agreement to help the therapist stick to the treatment plan obtained. Otherwise, the therapist and the physician may work at cross-purposes. If the physician feels that the patient is forcing his or her hand to arrange hospitalization, communication between therapist and physician will of course be necessary to make sure both are singing the same tune and to avoid "splitting."

Psychiatrists who treat patients with BPD using medication need to be adept at not allowing a patient to incorporate medication into self-destructive acting out, regardless of whether or not it is they who are also providing the psychotherapy. Let us look at some of the ways that physicians can accomplish this important treatment goal.

The physician should of course take a complete and detailed psychiatric history from the patient. This includes a review of Axis I symptoms. However, making an Axis I diagnosis in patients with BPD is not as straightforward an affair as it is with most other psychiatric patients. Patients may describe symptoms in a misleading manner or exhibit an atypical clinical presentation. Nor is their response to pharmacotherapy typical of other psychiatric patients. Clinicians need to be on the lookout for information that might call a seemingly straightforward diagnosis into question.

For example, a patient may complain of mood swings in a way that suggests bipolar disorder. On specific questioning, however, patients may admit that these "swings" last for 1 or 2 hours rather than for extended periods. The mood swings of bipolar disorder are not of such a short duration. So called *rapid cycling* bipolar patients are those who have several episodes per year, not per day. The patient may also say or believe that their dramatic mood changes are not initiated by environmental or interpersonal factors—a clinical presentation suggestive of true bipolar disorder—only to later describe in detail repetitive ongoing interactions that invariably trigger the swings. In such instances, it will be a part of the psychotherapists' task early in therapy to demonstrate to the patient that this connection is present. If two clinicians are involved, communication between the psychiatrist and the therapist about what the patient says at different times will circumvent many potential problems.

Patients who describe rage reactions should be quizzed specifically about panic symptoms. Rage reactions commonly are either preceded by or turn into panic attacks. The patient may not volunteer specific information about panic symptoms unless asked explicitly.

A good percentage of patients with BPD present with long-term dysthymic symptoms that occasionally rise to the level of a major depression. The pattern of sleep and appetite disturbance during such a depression will vary widely over time and is seldom consistent for lengthy periods. During an initial history, BPD patients may say that they have consistent disturbances of sleep, appetite, and energy, but the symptoms quickly disappear once the patient is hospitalized or commits to psychotherapy. Symptoms of a true major depression do not evaporate in such a manner. Seeing the patient several times within a relatively short period is a must in order to avoid misdiagnoses made on a cross-sectional presentation. Such patients are not lying about how they feel, but are giving global impressionistic descriptions of their symptoms. The clinician must have a high index of suspicion about what patients report while at the same time avoiding invalidation of the patient's perceptions. Just as with bipolar disorder, the physician must try to pin the patient down with specific questions regarding the time course of the symptoms before assuming that the patient has a major depression.

With the patient's permission, questioning other family members who have observed the patient over time may also help pin down the time course of any symptoms. However, one must keep in mind that the families of patients with BPD do not always give an accurate report either. At times they have a vested interest in establishing the presence of a condition like bipolar disorder, which they believe absolves them of any responsibility for the patient's condition, or they too may give their impressions and judgments rather than recite facts.

The physician must act like a good investigative reporter and question the patient and the family in a tactful manner about any inconsistencies in their stories. He or she must also be adept at spotting cleverly disguised or mentioned-in-passing hints that there may be information contradictory to the clinical presentation that the doctor is observing, and pursuing all such leads.

The chronic dysthymic symptoms of the BPD patient often have a completely different response to antidepressant medication from other forms of depression. Tricyclics have little effect. MAO inhibitors and serotonin reuptake inhibitor drugs (SSRIs) seem to help somewhat, with the latter being preferred because of their relative safety in overdose, lack of dietary restrictions, and lower number of side effects.

Although SSRIs often lead to a decrease in the BPD patient's general depression, they also seem to have the clinically useful effect of damping down the emotional reactivity of BPD patients (Coccaro & Kavoussi, 1997). The medications "raise the bar," so to speak, so that it takes a higher level of environmental stress to lead to an emotionally dysregulated state such as a rage attack or an episode of dissociation accompanied by self mutilation. SSRIs are also useful because they have the direct effect of decreasing the frequency of compulsive self-destructive behavior such as self-induced vomiting or self-cutting. If a long acting benzodiazepine is added, this effect may be augmented. These medications may sometimes eliminate such symptoms completely, although most patients will continue to exhibit the behaviors at reduced frequency and severity, and some will be completely untouched.

As of this writing, many psychiatrists have been using anticonvulsant medication to treat the BPD patient's unstable mood, regardless of whether or not they also diagnose the patient as bipolar I or II. The reasoning behind this strategy seems to be that if these drugs are useful in one kind of unstable mood (i.e., true bipolar disorder), they must be useful in other kinds. It may turn out that anticonvulsants are a useful adjunct in the treatment of unstable affect in patients with BPD, but thus far there are no more than a handful of case reports to back up their use, and no studies comparing their efficacy relative to SSRIs.

In patients with BPD, *no medicine works consistently*. I have found that if the family disturbances in these patients heat up to a certain degree, which is different for each patient, the symptoms of emotional dysregulation break through. As mentioned, SSRIs raise the threshold, but do not stop the reactions if things get bad enough. This phenomenon accounts for an apparent lack of a consistent response to medication by BPD patients, which in turn contributes to these patients' general reputation for distorting their symptoms for manipulative purposes.

Patients with BPD may abuse drugs episodically, which may lead some physicians to eschew the use of useful but potentially abusable drugs such as benzodiazepines. Sometimes doctors will even withhold clearly indicated medication, using potential drug abuse as an excuse, to "punish" BPD patients for their troubling behavior. More than once my patients who cut themselves severely have been refused pain medication. The thinking seems to be that somehow the infliction of pain by the physician will reduce the frequency of pain seeking behavior. It does not; in fact, it may increase it.

Benzodiazepines are in my opinion exceedingly benign drugs; their dangers are often grossly overstated. About the only consistent problems with them are that they can be habit forming—although the longer-acting agents are far less so than shorter acting ones— and that they may have street value, however slight. If the patient is found to be abusing the drugs, the psychiatrist can simply stop prescribing them. Little if any harm will have been done. On the other hand, as mentioned, benzodiazepines can add to the positive effects of SSRIs, and can stop panic attacks cold.

When patients with BPD abuse drugs, which they often do, it is usually done episodically and somewhat unpredictably compared to the steady usage of other drug addicts. As with other drug abusers, they may minimize their drug use, but they may also exaggerate it. For example, one patient claimed to have been taking a whopping dose of benzodiazepines, but all of her drug screens came back negative. When confronted with the discrepancy, she continued to insist that she was taking the pills—perhaps, she said, she had an absorption problem. To further complicate the picture, she would *act* like a drug addict. She would repeatedly phone in asking for refills just after 5 PM on nights when she knew a new doctor was covering for her usual doctor, and she used multiple pharmacies. When the on-call doctor questioned her about this practice, she became incensed that he would dare imply that she might be a drug addict. It was fascinating to me, although not surprising, that most physicians with whom she had come in contact continued to label her as "drug-seeking" despite their having obtained several negative drug screens. This patient's persona was partly predicated on the proposition that all physicians were bastards.

Another patient was thought to be a drug abuser because she always took more of a benzodiazepine than was prescribed. Her doctor had given her a very low dosage for what the doctor thought to be mild anxiety, but she had neglected to tell her doctor about her panic attacks. After finally becoming aware of the attacks, the physician raised the dosage of the medicine to the usual therapeutic levels for panic disorder. After that, the patient no longer took more medication than prescribed. She had been doing that before because she had not been receiving an adequate dosage. She made it appear however, that she was a difficult patient with a serious drug problem.

When prescribing any medication, the psychiatrist should discuss the indications for medication, give a rationale for its use (e.g., hypothalamic dysfunction of some sort in genetically prone individuals), and address any patient concerns or resistances. If patients continue to refuse appropriate medication after all resistances have been explored, psychotherapy can nonetheless be initiated or continued. If symptoms later interfere with the process of therapy, the therapist should express concerns that therapy may not be effective if the patient is preoccupied with symptoms yet continues to refuse symptomatic treatment.

Not infrequently, a patient with BPD will incorporate medication into a power struggle with the psychiatrist. Dawson (1988; Dawson & MacMillan, 1993) has described a useful technique for such a situation. The psychiatrist deliberately downplays expectancies regarding the medications. He or she might say, "I think this is worth a try; it may work, it may not." If the patient insists on changes in the dose or the kind of medication, the therapist may offer an opinion that the patient should stick with the current medication. If the patient continues to insist on a change, and the requested change is not a dangerous one, the doctor acquiesces. If asked for an inappropriate medication such as a narcotic, the therapist politely says, "I'm not willing to do that because it's not indicated." If patients continue to object, the physician can tell them sincerely that he or she will not be offended if they want to obtain another opinion.

OTHER SYMPTOMATIC TREATMENTS

Linehan (1993) developed a training manual for patients with BPD that teaches various stress management techniques. In her dialectical behavior therapy (DBT), a treatment that has some significant commonalties with unified therapy, these skills are taught in a group-therapy milieu that is used alongside of her individual psychotherapy sessions and is meant to complement them. However, studies using a dismantling strategy have thus far suggested that the skills training component is not DBT's active ingredient (Scheel, 2000).

Nonetheless, some patients benefit greatly from one or another of the techniques. Dr. Linehan allows handouts describing the exercises to be photocopied from her skills training manual. The handouts can then be given to patients. The patient can try some of them out without necessarily participating in group therapy. When patients who are responding poorly to medications or who are demanding something else that is quick and simple to help control emotional dysregulation, I will offer the handouts.

When I give out this material, I often find that patients have already been taught about these exercises in a previous therapy or have thought of some of them on their own. The techniques do seem to help, but once again not consistently. I find that presenting them using Dawson's approach often defuses spoiling responses and paradoxically increases the usefulness of the manual. I downplay my hopes for their success by saying, "Try some of these out if you haven't already; they may help or they may not."

SELF-MUTILATION

Persistent self-mutilation in a nonpsychotic patient is the closest thing there is to a pathognomonic sign for the diagnosis of BPD. It remains one of the most baffling and frustrating of all psychiatric symptoms. Various theories about its symbolic value to the patients or the messages that the patients intend to communicate thought the behavior have been offered (Conterio & Lader, 1998); thus far, I have not found any of these explanations completely convincing.

Self-mutilation, after it has started, may later be incorporated by the patient into spoiling behavior. However, in most cases the goals of the spoiling could have been produced using less drastic techniques. When asked why they self-mutilate, the one answer most consistently given by patients with BPD is that the behavior reduces their anxiety. Indirect evidence that the behavior leads to the release of endorphins (an endogenous opiate) supports that contention. Why or how such a biological mechanism was selected for during evolution is unclear. It may possibly have something to do with the inherited tendency of people to sacrifice themselves for the good of the group. It can be seen in "normal" cultures in several forms, such as certain circumcision rituals and, in some Moslem societies, a holiday in which men parade down the street slashing their foreheads with razor blades.

While we do not know the actual cause of the behavior, in many instances we can figure out what interpersonal relationship patterns tend to *trigger* it. The details vary with each patient, but the overall situation seems to be similar in many cases: Patients who self-mutilate are often in the middle of a situation in which they feel a desperate need to find an immediate, effective response to double-binding family behavior, while at the same time feeling completely helpless and at a loss for how to accomplish this goal. Their anxiety crescendos to unspeakably high levels, and only the act of hurting themselves seems to decrease it. We see the same phenomenon to a milder degree in men who get so frustrated that they put their fist through a wall. The origin of the expression "I'm pulling my hair over this" may also lie in this process.

Early in therapy, the therapist has no idea about precisely what the family has done or is doing when the patient feels this anxiety surge; nor does the therapist have a clue about the best strategy for the patient to use with the family for putting a stop to it. Later on in therapy, after a strategy has been developed, the therapist can respond to a patient's distress call with specific suggestions or with additional coaching.

The best thing the therapist has to offer for self-mutilation early in therapy is medications that reduce the anxiety crescendo, with or without supplementation with self-soothing and stress management techniques. If the therapist attempts to make other glib suggestions about how the patient might stop hurting himself or herself, the patient's spoiling behavior (including increased self-mutilation) is actually likely to *increase*. It does so because the patient knows full well that the therapist in reality is clueless as to what is going on, but is trying to "help" anyway. This is a recreation of a common family dynamic, and the patient responds accordingly.

As mentioned, when a patient calls me early in therapy with a desperate question on how he or she should handle an impossible problem, I will usually declare my own helplessness, so that the patient does not feel a need to feed into it. I might say, "I sure wish I knew enough to give you some advice on that question. It's a kind of catch-22; it takes time to find out what is creating this problem but in the meantime you're stuck with it. What a horrible bind." The patient may respond that the therapist should have figured it out by then, to which the therapist can reply, "Perhaps so. We're working on it. I wish I had something quick and easy."

The patient may then ask the therapist what to do about the anxiety. The therapist can inquire about what medications or techniques the patient has already tried that have worked in the past, or offer some the patient has not yet tried. However, with one exception, the therapist should not offer any other suggestions for the reasons just described. The one exception, I have recently found, is that some patients can be advised that they probably *do not have to do anything*. The therapist can say, "From the little I know about your situation, the problem creating the feeling will probably go away and be replaced by another one in relatively short order. It probably won't make much difference in the long run how you respond now." This statement resonates with the patient's experience and can at times be soothing.

Ultimately, if the client's anxiety is high enough, nothing will stop self-mutilation at that particular instant. The therapist must learn to live with that uncomfortable knowledge. In Linehan's DBT, discussing the patient's self-mutilation takes a high priority. Although I agree that it must be addressed to the extent possible, I have also found that discussing it in therapy ad nauseum may also be used by the patient as a resistance to describing and learning about how to handle the family interactions that trigger it in the first place. If the behavior is mild and not overly disfiguring, I am comfortable with proceeding with the central therapy strategies and not paying excessive attention to it.

Certainly, the therapist should not reward self-mutilation with extra sessions or phone conversations; Linehan's suggestion that the therapist refuse to talk to a patient immediately after the act is a useful one. Hospitalization for this behavior, in my opinion, actually reinforces the behavior and is therefore contraindicated unless the patient forces the therapist's hand.

ACQUISITION OF A COMPLETE SOCIAL HISTORY

Before recommending psychotherapy for a particular patient, the therapist should have a minimal outline of the patient's life story and relationship history. The following information should be obtained during the initial evaluatory sessions in an empathic but matter of fact, leaving-no-stone-unturned style of questioning:

1. Parents and/or stepparents: Are they living? Are they still together? When, if they are separated or divorced, did this take place? Did they get along with each other? Did either of them

have any previous marriages? Is there a family history of mental illness? How did the patient get along with each parent? How did the family get along in general when the patient was growing up?

2. Siblings: How many are there? What were their birth order, age range, and genders? What is their current marital and career status? If the patient is an only child, does the patient know why the parents did not have more children?

3. Family violence or abuse: The patient should be questioned directly about this issue. In general, the patient is asked if there any was physical, sexual, or psychological abuse. Was there any violence in the family, and if so, who did what to whom? This discussion need not go into specific details at this point if the patient seems uncomfortable.

4. History of overtly self-damaging acts, such as wrist cutting, self mutilation, self-induced vomiting, suicide threats or gestures.

5. Educational history: How far did the patient get in school? What sort of grades did the patient get?

6. Employment history: What jobs did the patient have? Were there periods of disability? If the patient changed jobs frequently, what were the reasons for that? Were there periods of unemployment?

7. Relationship history: Has the patient had any long-term relationships? Marriages? Divorces? Were there any recurrent patterns or themes (e.g., involvement with abusive spouses, alcoholics, partners who do not work, or cheaters)? Who is generally dominant in these relationships? Was a career or other goal interrupted by a relationship?

8. Ethnic and religious background of the family.

RECOMMENDATION FOR PSYCHOTHERAPY AND OFFERING AN INITIAL TREATMENT FRAME

The next step in the early sessions of therapy is for the therapist, based on his or her assessment of the entire history obtained from the patient, to recommend psychotherapy as the treatment of choice for the patient's chief complaints. The patient's complaints should be framed in a way that provides a basic rationale for the recommendation for psychotherapy. In unified therapy, the basic frame usually involves one or more of the following themes: chronic affective symptoms of unknown or unclear etiology, a pattern of self-destructive or self-defeating behavior, or overt family discord with which the patient is having difficulty coping. The therapist should use some variation on the following basic intervention:

"When someone [is feeling anxious or depressed and is not sure exactly why] [is having family problems and cannot seem to solve them] [finds themselves doing things repetitively that are making them feel bad], psychotherapy is indicated to try to figure out exactly what is happening and what can be done about it. I recommend that we meet weekly—or every other week if finances are a problem—to do that."

The patient, of course, has the option of agreeing to therapy or not agreeing to it. If the patient does not agree, the therapist should tactfully inquire as to the patient's reasons, and attempt to address his or her concerns. If the patient still refuses, the therapist should express concern that the patient may not resolve the problem, but should not try to badger the patient into changing his or her mind. Coming to therapy should always be more important for the client than it is for the therapist. Motivating a client to change is hard enough when he or she is committed to the process. If clients say they want to "try again on my own," the therapist should sincerely wish them well on this endeavor, and leave the door open for them to return if they should change their minds.

If the patient agrees to therapy, the therapist goes on to offer a description of how therapy proceeds, again checking for any concerns or reluctance the patient may have about that process. Before discussing that, I would first like to address the problem of managed-care restrictions on psychotherapy.

MANAGED CARE RESTRICTIONS
ON PSYCHOTHERAPY

It can safely be said that at present there are no short-term psychotherapies that are effective for the treatment of any severe personality disorder. Habits that have been molded and reinforced by powerful forces almost from birth do not change quickly. Managed-care insurance companies know this. They know that patients will not even tell the therapist what the real issues are until the patient has formed a trusting relationship with the therapist. However, insurance companies have an inherent conflict of interest. Their primary goal is maximize profits for their CEOs and shareholders. If patients are helped through their activities, all the better, but if not, insurance companies are concerned only to the extent that they may lose customers to competing plans. This attitude has prevailed in managed care more than in other similar businesses because some large insurance companies have had legal protection against being assessed punitive damages for their misbehavior in a court of law. Fortunately, as of this writing this protection is quickly being eroded.

On the other hand, of course, the health needs of the general population are not served if resources are drained by therapists who are unconcerned with costs and efficacy. For this reason, any techniques that can be used to shorten therapy should be employed. Unified therapy aims for brie*fer* therapy, but there are natural limitations to how short the process of therapy can become. Personality disorders are by no means trivial conditions; their cost in terms of patient morbidity and mortality are astronomical. They are certainly as worthy of treatment as, say, a gall bladder problem. Most surgical procedures are considerably more expensive than 1 year of psychotherapy.

It is important to discuss with patients the limitations of their insurance and the fact that the cost of effective treatment may exceed their coverage; the therapist should maintain, however, that any additional costs are well worth paying for. Many if not most patients can come up with the money if they have to; they often waste considerable resources on their own self-destructive behavior such as using drugs or gambling. Because the patient's family indirectly benefits from his or her treatment, I also see no inherent problem in letting them pay for it if necessary.

Managed-care reviewers have employed a number of different tactics to avoid covering the cost of treatment of patients with BPD without admitting that that is what they are doing. Some will simply say, "We don't cover treatment for this condition." This may at least be an honest response. It is perfectly reasonable for insurance companies to set policy for what they will and will not cover, although I believe it is part of the responsibility of therapists to lobby for coverage of effective psychotherapy. However, in many cases the insurance company will only make this statement to the therapist, not to the patient. After all, the patient might complain to an employer about insurance coverage or look for a better plan.

The simple answer to the reviewer in such a case should be, "All right, I will let the patient know that you do not cover treatment for her problem, and that if she wishes to have it, she will have to pay for it out of her own pocket." Not infrequently, the insurance company will then back down and authorize some sessions. I strongly recommend that therapists do not sign any contract that precludes their providing treatment for noncovered services at the patient's own expense, or that prohibits therapists from telling a patient that they do not agree with the company's determination of medical necessity. Such clauses are put into contracts so that the insurance company can lie to its policyholders about what really is covered and what is not.

Another managed care mainstay is to indirectly imply that a therapist who wants authorization for longer-term treatments is somehow incompetent, dishonest, or not up to date on the latest solution-oriented treatment strategies. The reviewers may subtly question the therapist's abilities. They may question his or her integrity by implying that the therapist is purposely running up the bill with unproven treatments. The therapist may feel that he or she is in danger of being kicked off the insurance company's provider panel. These tactics are meant to intimidate therapists from asking for more sessions. The managed care company also wants patients to go away thinking that they have been given all that can be done for their condition, so they do not complain.

The recommended response here is for the therapist to become familiar with the current literature about the disorder and politely remind the reviewer that BPD is not amenable to short-term treatment but that, although the prognosis is not terrific, patients can certainly improve significantly with current treatments. It is also important to outline what the therapist's specific treatment goals are and how he or she plans to achieve them, in order to reassure the insurer that the therapist is not engaging in an interminable approach with an unclear end point. In my experience, enlightened companies often authorize sessions if the therapist appears confident of his or her position and can offer a specific plan. Fortunately, the methods and goals of unified therapy can be described very specifically and concretely, and mesh nicely with the preference of insurance company for "solution oriented" treatment. If the behavior of an insurance company clearly indicates complete disregard for patient welfare, it behooves us all to refuse to continue working with it.

Another useful response is the "pay me now, or pay me a lot more later" approach. The therapist tactfully reminds the reviewer that therapy can help reduce both the overall likelihood and most certainly the frequency of expensive psychiatric hospitalizations for BPD patients.

To my mind, any therapist who agrees to limit treatment to a few sessions without informing the patient that this treatment will in all likelihood be grossly inadequate is unethical. The need to stay on a certain insurance panel is no excuse; despite what they may imply, insurance companies need providers as much as providers need insurance companies. No cardiac surgeon would agree to a contract that said, "If there are complications during the heart bypass surgery you are providing, don't treat them. Additional treatment is too expensive. We want to pay our CEOs a higher salary. Be sure to lie to the patient about their having received adequate treatment."

DESCRIPTION OF THE PROCESS OF THERAPY

After obtaining the patient's agreement to begin a course of psychotherapy, the therapist educates the patient on the basic process of therapy. Patients are told precisely what the therapist expects them to do at the beginning of therapy. Potential therapy interfering behaviors on the part of the patient are brought up for discussion, and the concept of resistance is introduced. In general, the therapist covers the following points:

First, as in psychoanalysis, the patient is instructed that therapy begins with a process of free association. The therapist tells patients that they should report all of their thoughts without censoring them in advance, as would be typical in most conversations. The therapist acknowledges that opening up this way is not easy insofar as the patient does not know the therapist, but that disclosure of all thoughts is the goal. Patients should try not to label their thoughts as irrelevant, embarrassing, or offensive to the therapist, but report everything that comes across their minds, *with a general focus on the previously identified problem areas.*

Unlike in psychoanalysis, the therapist does not want the client to free associate about just any thing that comes to mind, but about the specific issues identified in the treatment frame. Unified therapy is a far more active treatment than psychoanalysis, but initially allowing the patient to develop a story with minimal interference from the therapist is an excellent way to gather essential information.

Second, the therapist tells the patient that initially the therapist will be relatively inactive, and will just ask questions about what the patient is saying. The patient is then told that, in relatively short order, the therapist will become more active with suggestions and homework assignments. The patient is informed that the therapist must understand quite a bit before being able to say anything helpful.

Spelling all of this out up front often undercuts the tendency of the patient with BPD to demand from therapists quick solutions based on limited information. Therapists can always say that they do not yet know enough to give any feedback. If the patient replies that somehow the therapist should be able to say more based on what has already been said, therapists can indicate, without a sarcastic tone of voice, that they wish they were quicker at being able to put a solution together for the patient. In any event, the therapist should always retain the option to listen and make no comments when the patient's situation is unclear.

Third, the therapist tells the client that it will often be difficult to discuss the very topics that are most important. Because the patient is coming in distress, a discussion of the issues that lead to the distress is itself distressing. It can be anxiety-provoking to talk about things the patient is anxious about, depressing to talk about things the patient is depressed about, and so on. The therapist then expresses a wish that he or she knew of away around this catch-22.

When these feelings occur, the therapist further explains, people have a natural tendency to want to avoid coming to therapy. They may find it difficult to come or they may miss sessions. For this reason, should the patient decide to quit therapy, he or she should return one last time to see if the therapist has struck a nerve. If the patient thinks the therapist is completely off track, this should be expressed to the therapist. The patient may be right, and the therapist may need to change course. Patients may or may not keep this part of the treatment contract. If they agree to it, however, the likelihood is increased that the therapist will get them to return if they abruptly call to discontinue therapy sessions. The therapist reminds them that they had agreed before to come back for one last session.

The therapist next asks patients about any questions they may have about the recommendation for therapy or the instructions. If a client seems reluctant to proceed, the therapist tactfully quizzes the client on the source of the reluctance. If a client expresses a concern in metaphor (e.g., describing some untoward event that happened to someone else, or describing how his or her relationships normally turn out poorly), the therapist should make a paradoxical prediction. As previously described, the therapist tells the client that the therapist is concerned that the client might at some point think that something similar is happening in therapy, and that he or she should bring it to the therapist's attention should those feelings pop up. If the patient goes on to state that the therapist's concern is unwarranted, the therapist should not argue, but answer, "OK, but let's keep an eye out for it."

If any time remains in the session, the therapist instructs the patient to begin talking. In the next chapter, we discuss therapy techniques useful in gathering information identifying interpersonal relationship patterns that cue self-destructive behavior or symptoms, and gathering information about the patient's genogram. We discuss how to offer a hypothesis about the patient's family dynamics and his or her role in it, and outline a solution for the patient's problems.

8

Exploration and Interpretation

The therapist's goal in the early part of unified therapy is to obtain accurate descriptions of the interpersonal relationship patterns within the patient's family that trigger his or her problematic symptoms or behavior. Once the problematic interactions are clearly identified, this focus naturally leads both the patient and the therapist to the question of why the family members behave the way they do. The therapist tries to arrive at an answer to this question by gathering genogram material that helps to explain the genesis of the problematic family patterns. The therapist's goal in doing so is to help the patient develop empathy for his or her family's noxious behavior. The therapist then goes on to present an initial working hypothesis to the patient about how his or her self-destructive role–function behavior seems to stabilize the family and why the family seems to need the patient to behave in such a manner.

Before discussing how therapy proceeds after the patient has agreed to the initial treatment contract, this chapter begins with a discussion of methods by which a therapist can avoid the so-called "distortions" for which the patient with BPD is notorious. We also discuss general strategies for achieving one other important goal in the early part of therapy: recruiting the patient's spouse or significant other, if any, as an ally in the patient's therapy, or at least encouraging the spouse not to interfere with therapy.

AVOIDING PATIENT DISTORTIONS

As mentioned earlier, patients with BPD have a reputation for distorted thinking about what transpires in their lives and using these supposed distortions to manipulate the therapist and, in the process, defeat the therapy. Although these patients certainly can and often do lead the therapist astray, I find it far more useful to believe that they really want therapy to work, and that their distortions are more apparent than real. In addition, at some level clients know they must be honest. They are ambivalent about change to be sure, but they would not come to therapy if they held out no hope for it.

I have found consistently that much of the BPD patient's apparent distortion evaporates if the therapist knows what questions to ask and how to ask them. My conviction in this regard comes from several sources. I have invited important family members into sessions and gotten their side of the story, and have even had some of them come back to me later for individual psychotherapy themselves. I have listened to taped telephone conversations between adult patients with BPD and their parents, and watched videotapes of family therapy sessions led by therapist trainees. I have also watched independently recorded videotapes of mothers and their adult borderline daughters, each in individual psychotherapy with different therapists, discussing their views about the very same examples of their interaction.

When first asked about a particular interactional relationship episode, patients with BPD often respond with a rather global judgment about the people involved rather than a specific description of what actually took place. A patient may, for example, describe her father as "controlling." Unless the therapist knows precisely what the patient means by "controlling," he or she is in no position to judge whether this characterization is accurate. A typical scenario in which a therapist might conclude that he or she is being misled might go something like this: The patient states globally to the therapist that her father tries to control whatever she does. Dad might, unbeknownst to the therapist, call her incessantly on her cell phone whenever she goes out on a date. On further inquiry, however, the therapist learns that the father bankrolls his daughter's every whim, no matter how reckless, whenever she asks him for money. The therapist then draws the incorrect conclusion that the patient's characterization of the father as "controlling" is distorted.

In order to avoid this scenario, it is important to find out exactly what behavior the father engages in that leads the patient to use the term *controlling*. In other words, what specific behaviors and suspected motives of the father are entailed by the patient's use of the term? Even people who most others would find very power-oriented do not try to control absolutely everything their family members do. They would not in most instances care, for example, what time family members brushed their teeth.

A therapist must be a good investigative reporter and ask for specifics using follow-up questions. In general, therapists should follow all interesting leads, ask for clarification of vague or confusing statements, ask for specific examples of misbehavior by other family members, and run down implied but unspoken implications. In the above case of a judgment masquerading as a description, the therapist should ask for illustrative examples. He or she could ask, "What exactly is your father trying to make you do or not do?" If the patient responds with another global generalization such as, "Everything!" the therapist persistently asks for some prototypical examples. After an example of an interaction is finally given, it may still be necessary to ask for further clarification: Exactly how did the father's behavior lead the patient to conclude that he wanted to control one of her activities? The father's statements as reported by the patient may sound relatively innocuous to the therapist, but such may not be the case. The therapist might ask, "What was it about that statement that made you think that he does not want you to get married?"

Another instance when follow-up questions are essential is in the case of a description masquerading as an explanation. This phenomenon usually occurs when a therapist asks patients to explain their motives for behaving in a certain fashion, or the reasons why they are fearful of some action, and in response they merely paraphrase an earlier description of their state of mind. The response sounds like an explanation for the motives or fears, but in fact explains nothing.

For example, a therapist might ask a patient whose career might be adversely affected why he or she is refusing to make an important business presentation. If the patient answers, "I am afraid of public speaking," the patient seems to be saying that he or she has a very common simple phobia, and that is all there is to it. After all, public speaking fears are common; almost anyone might be completely paralyzed by them. What remains unexplained, however, is both the true source of the patient's anxiety, and the reasons why the patient has not yet done anything to remedy it. As we know from cognitive therapy, there is usually an underlying assessment of what might happen in a feared situation. What is it? If the feared consequence the patient reports is highly unlikely, what makes the patient focus on it? In addition, successful business people who have troubles with public speaking will usually search actively for solutions; they may ask for medication, practice speaking at Toastmasters, read books about others who have overcome similar troubles, and so forth. What has the patient done?

On hearing a patient volunteer a pseudo-explanation, the therapist should pursue the questions of what thoughts the phobia is based on and what the patient has done previously to get over the phobia. If the problem is long-standing and the patient has done nothing about it until going to therapy, what exactly has been stopping him or her? If the patient says, "I just didn't think there was anything I could do about it," the therapist should inquire if the patient had even looked into possible solutions, and if not, why not.

Another common example of a description masquerading as an explanation takes the form of "I don't do such and such because I don't like doing that." This "explanation" might refer to essential activities such as getting retrained for alternate employment after being laid off ("I just don't like school") or having long-term relationships ("I prefer to be alone"). In this case, the patient seems to be saying that the decision is just a matter of personal taste, like preferring black suits to blue ones. The fallacy here is that the patient is comparing decisions made on the basis of personal idiosyncrasies to those that are made on the basis of weighing the pros and cons of a specific course of action. The therapist needs to ask specifically what the pros and cons are that went into the patient's decision, and what makes the patient give a lot of weight to some of them and little weight to others.

Another technique helpful in avoiding globalized judgments and obtaining accurate descriptions of family relationship patterns from BPD patients involves asking specifically who said exactly what to whom. Patients who may otherwise omit important details often are able to provide quite accurate recollections of emotion-laden conversations. An important caveat is that the therapist needs to get the whole conversation, not just the beginning of it. The therapist needs to be alert to whether or not he or she has an understanding of the upshot of the conversation. Useful questions in this regard include, "What did *you* say after he said that?" "How did he respond to that?" and "How did the conversation end? Did he just walk away without saying anything?"

The more specific and detailed the questions the therapist asks, the more accurate the picture of the patient's relationships becomes. Of course, some patients can obfuscate the picture by giving too much detail so that the trees obscure the forest. Some patients will go on and give example after example until way past the time when therapists already know all they need to know. The patient may do so in order to avoid taking the next steps of therapy because of anxiety over the frightening task of trying to stop the dysfunctional interactions. The therapist can interrupt such a process by tactfully pointing out that he or she already has sufficient examples to understand the problem at hand.

If the patient seems reluctant to give concrete examples of family interactions, the therapist needs to make a clinical judgment about how hard to push for them. In the first few sessions of therapy, it is probably wise to push a little but to back off if the patient resists, because the patient has not yet decided whether or not the therapist is trustworthy. The therapist should say, "Well, we can come back to that later." It is important to indicate to the patient that the therapist is not avoiding subjects that make the patient anxious. I have found that after the seventh or eighth session I can use the anxiety-provoking technique (Sifneos, 1992) of staying on the subject until the patient opens up. The therapist can say, "I know this is hard to talk about, but it sounds really important."

Accepting the Patient's Reactions to the Therapist's Hypotheses. In the early stages of psychotherapy, patients with BPD are usually reluctant to explicitly declare feelings and thoughts that are, unbeknownst to the therapist, unacceptable in their family system. They will not be willing to do so unless they have some minimal level of faith that the therapist not only understands their dilemma, but is also trustworthy. On the other hand, they also know that the therapist will not be able to help them unless they do communicate these thoughts and feelings. In this situation, a common psychotherapy error inadvertently plays into the tendency of patients with BPD to portray themselves as cognitively impaired or unreasonably manipulative. Iatrogenic induction of such a clinical picture is yet another way in which a therapist can be misled about the capabilities and very nature of these patients.

Because of the bind they feel themselves to be in, BPD patients may imply that they have certain thoughts and feelings, but if asked directly deny that they do. Novice therapists, particularly those who think it important for clients to "get in touch with their feelings," often make the mistake of insisting on direct verbal agreement. For example, patients may complain vociferously about a particular relative, but deny harboring any feelings of anger toward him or her. In spite of the denial, they may then start listing additional complaints, but are cut off by a therapist who tries to get them to "see" that they are "in denial." The usual result is that the patient does express anger—at the therapist.

Whenever the therapist presents a hypothesis about the client's affects, thoughts, conflicts, or relationship patterns, he or she can save much time and transference reactivity by avoiding this pitfall. The therapist should not insist on direct verbal agreement if the patient implies agreement. That is, if instead of overtly agreeing, the client goes on to give further examples or memories consistent with the therapist's guess, the therapist must not press the patient for overt agreement. For example, if the therapist says, "You must be furious with your Dad," and the patient responds with additional complaints about him, the therapist should take this as a sign that the patient agrees with the therapist's assessment. There is no need for further comment; the therapist need only remain silent and listen for more details.

If patients overtly disagree with the therapist's assessment yet continue to offer confirmatory material, the therapist might or might not tactfully point this out, but again, must not insist that the guess is correct. If patients disagree and do not go on, the therapist should attempt to clarify in what respect the hypothesis is incorrect. If patients agree with the therapist merely to please him or her, this will eventually be revealed by inconsistencies and incongruities in the patient's story.

KEEPING THE SPOUSE INFORMED

Spouses and significant others have long been notorious for making a psychotherapist's life difficult by interfering with, and in some cases actively subverting, the therapist's work with the patient. Usually this phenomenon has been conceptualized as the unreasonable act of a fellow dysfunctional individual, who really ought to be in therapy himself or herself. If, on the other hand, we start with the assumption that, like the patient, the spouse is acting reasonably, we must then ask what the good reasons are for the spouse's objections to the therapist's treatment plan. In unified therapy with patients with BPD, this is even more essential than in other psychotherapy models. The spouse almost invariably causes problems if his or her objections are not properly understood and addressed.

There are usually three main reasons why spouses object to the recommendations of unified therapists. The first and second reasons are related to the marital quid pro quo described in Part One. When the patient and spouse began their relationship, they made an implicit deal that they would help one another maintain certain role functions derived from their positions in their respective families of origin. The unified therapist is in essence asking one member of the couple to renege on the deal! The therapist is telling the patient to say to the spouse, in effect, that the spouse's services as an accomplice are no longer necessary, and that the patient will stop being an accomplice for the spouse. This creates problems for the spouse on two fronts.

First, the spouse becomes very confused about how to behave around the patient. This happens because the mutual expectations within the relationship had up until then been exceedingly rigid, as well as perhaps familiar from the spouse's own family of origin. Suddenly, everything is seemingly up for renegotiations. This was not what the spouse signed up for. Worse yet, the spouse can never be completely sure that the requested change is really what the patient wants in the first place. This uncertainty is due to the "game without end" phenomenon that is discussed later in the book. Furthermore, if the spouse had performed the marital quid pro quo services for the patient at great personal sacrifice, as is so often the case, the spouse becomes angry thinking that the sacrifice had been unnecessary and unappreciated all along. Second, the patient's new behavior will probably no longer be helpful to the spouse in maintaining his or her role behavior within the spouse's own family of origin. Ambivalent as they may be, the husbands or wives are not themselves in therapy, and feel in no position to challenge their own family, although they probably do not think of the problem in those terms.

In short, patients in unified therapy may no longer act in ways helpful for reinforcing a spouse's persona, and may no longer want the spouse to act out that persona for them. If this eventuality is not addressed properly by the therapist, the spouse will invariably feel utterly betrayed. In fact, if a patient ever uses the word *betrayed* in discussing the spouse, or attributes its usage to the spouse, the therapist can rest assured that the patient is referring to an unexpected violation of the marital quid pro quo.

The third reason for spousal interference comes into play later in therapy. The spouse often vehemently objects to the therapist's recommendation that patients metacommunicate with their family of origin. The spouse may appear to do so out of some evil or neurotic need to "keep the patient in his or her place," but the real reason is usually far more benign: The spouse has most likely witnessed previously unsuccessful efforts by the patient to address family issues, after which the patient became an emotional wreck. The spouse was the one left to pick up the pieces. It is hardly surprising that the spouse would find the therapist's recommendation pure folly. This problem is handled by the therapist's finding ways to reassure the spouse that the therapist is aware of the dangers associated with metacommunication and is planning a strategy that will circumvent such disastrous results. How this is achieved is described in the next chapter when detriangulating strategies are addressed.

Addressing the issue of the marital quid pro quo is a bit more complicated. In order to prevent the patient's significant other from feeling betrayed, the therapist should instruct patients who are in committed romantic relationships to keep the spouse or partner informed about everything that transpires in therapy. In particular, partners should be told about any insights the patient has gained about family dynamics and the patient's role in them. Therapists should give this instruction even if marital issues do not seem to be directly related to the patient's complaints. The therapist should occasionally check with the patient to see if this instruction is being carried out. The therapist should also ask the patient from time to time about what comments the spouse is making about the patient's therapy.

If a patient refuses to discuss therapy with the partner, the patient's reasons for the refusal should be explored. The therapist should also express to the patient concern that refusal to keep the spouse informed about therapy might lead the spouse to attempt to interfere with what the patient and therapist are trying to accomplish.

If the patient and spouse have an abusive or chaotic relationship, or one characterized by poor communications skills, it may be difficult for the patient to keep the spouse informed about therapy without exacerbating marital problems. For this reason, it may become necessary for the therapist to coach the patient on how to metacommunicate with the spouse, particularly about how their respective families of origins have affected their relationship with each other. Devising strategies for accomplishing this aim as well as teaching the patient to effectively employ those strategies is accomplished using the same role-playing methods that are used to teach family-of-origin metacommunication. These methods are also described in the next chapter.

Because marital and family-of-origin issues are so interconnected, and because the patient's parents and spouse interact with each other as well as with the patient, the question frequently arises as to which relationship issues to tackle first: problems with the parents or problems with the spouse. There is no hard and fast rule for prioritizing these therapeutic goals. It is often necessary to go back and forth between teaching the patient how to talk with the spouse and teaching the patient how to talk with the parents. A danger here is that the patient may switch back and forth between talking in therapy about these relationships in such a manner that precludes resolution of issues in *any* of the relationships. Much sensitivity and therapy skill is required for striking the proper balance.

Fortunately, if the patient is ready for change, the spouse often is as well. Enlistment of the spouse as an ally rather than an adversary is the most frequent result if the therapist handles the matter well. As the patient's therapy proceeds, the spouse often gains insight into his or her own family-of-origin issues, and may even decide to go into therapy to address them. It is also possible, however, that any change by the patient may be completely unacceptable to the spouse, and a divorce threat may ensue. In the latter case, the patient may decide that the loss of that relationship is an unacceptable price to pay, even if it means that the patient will continue in a highly dysfunctional and unsatisfying life style. The patient may prefer to stop therapy. In such instances, the therapist may advocate for continued psychotherapy somewhat by reviewing with the patient the consequences of different courses of action. The ultimate choice belongs of course to the patient.

GETTING PSYCHOTHERAPY STARTED

After the treatment contract has been agreed to, the "rules" of therapy explained, and the patient's concerns about the process addressed, the therapist tells the patient to go ahead and start talking about his or her thoughts. Patients with BPD generally launch into their usual complaints without too much difficulty or prompting from the therapist. If the patient has difficulty initiating a session, the therapist may employ any of the usual techniques from psychodynamic or experiential psychotherapy to help the patient open up.

As the patient reveals his or her thoughts or attempts to engage the therapist in some other way, therapists quietly perform a variety of tasks. They listen for the transference traps discussed in chapter 6 and react accordingly. They validate the patient as much as possible by agreeing with anything that they can agree with while ignoring any added hyperbole or loaded statements. They also listen for information that elucidates the patient's core interpersonal relationship schemata, particularly those about which the patient is conflicted. The conflicts will later be interpreted to the patient as conflicts between the patient's idiosyncratic or self-actualizing desires, and apparent family-of-origin demands for specific role behavior. For patients with BPD, the therapist looks primarily for references to conflicts over autonomy, and identifies the specific areas of the patient's life to which the conflicts pertain, such as career ambitions or romantic relationships. The therapist also listens for manifestations of spoiling behavior, references to the patient's feeling invalidated or blamed for something for which he or she is not responsible, self-denigrating thoughts, and descriptions of risky behavior.

In the beginning of therapy, unless specifically cornered by the patient into describing what they think the most important variables triggering his or her problems are likely to be, unified therapists do not declare biases overtly about the central role of family-of-origin behavior. The therapist merely listens as the patient describes typical relationship episodes, which are defined by Luborsky and Crits-Christoph (1990) as "… a part of a session that occurs as a relatively discreet episode of explicit narration about relationships with others or with the self" (p. 16). Patients are extremely likely to describe such episodes. Luborsky and others (1990) have found that, in the average psychotherapy session, relatively complete relationship episodes are described naturally an average of 4.1 times, with a range from 1 to 7.

Whenever the patient brings up interactions with others, the therapist perks up and, as previously described, asks questions designed to clarify what takes place within the interactions. The therapist pays particularly close attention when the patient brings up interactions with family members.

Of course, the fact that the therapist pays particular attention to family of origin issues will eventually reveal the therapist's biases. The patient will no doubt figure out what the therapist expects to hear. I believe that followers of any theory will reveal biases in such a manner and that it is impossible to proceed in psychotherapy without a theory. Therefore, it is impossible for a therapist to have no effect on what type of information the patient volunteers in the therapy session. Fortunately, when clients make up stories only to please the therapist, the stories tend to become incoherent or inconsistent. This signals to honest therapists that their biases may be leading the patient into providing them with inaccurate information.

As they listen to descriptions of relationship episodes, therapists look for recurring themes and conflicts. The identification of conflictual themes can be made using techniques borrowed from a variety of therapy schools. Luborsky and Crits-Christoph's (1990) Core Conflictual Relationship Theme (CCRT) method is very useful. The therapist can also look for polarized or inflexible behavior (Allen, 1988), motivational ambiguity (Allen, 1991), seemingly irrational reasoning (Allen, 1988, 1991), or the "markers" of emotional processing problems described by Greenberg, Rice, and Elliot (1993).

As problematic or conflictual themes emerge, the therapist gradually develops the idea with patients that their chief complaint and other problems are shaped, triggered, and reinforced by certain behavior by important family-of-origin members. Chronic or recurring problems in other relationships, such as with peers, spouses, or employers, are similarly framed as shaped, triggered, and reinforced by certain behaviors by the family.

TYING PATIENT COMPLAINTS
TO FAMILY OF ORIGIN ISSUES

In my experience, the vast majority of issues that patients bring up in therapy relate in some way to core conflictual family-of-origin themes. The therapist can therefore try to connect, if possible, almost anything the patient says to family-of-origin issues. If a patient is tangential, the tangent itself usually relates in some way to these core issues, and can be used to reconnect to them. If the patient digresses on to temporary problems, the therapist should attempt to find parallels between such problems and the relevant family dynamics, and to eventually show the patient why family issues prevent or make difficult resolution of the described difficulties. In this section, we look at some strategies that allow therapists to gradually clarify the patient's family dynamics and to develop for the patient a family-of-origin hypothesis that explains the patient's chief complaints in a way that is palatable to him or her.

Reframing. Reframing is defined as attaching a positive or adaptive motivation to any significant family member's actions or characteristics that a patient has branded as bad or undesirable. In unified therapy, the reframed motive is eventually used to relate the action or characteristic of the person to some sort of family pattern. To illustrate how this is done, let us look first at how the therapist might handle the question of who is to blame for the patient's problems.

Although patients with personality disorders are notorious for blaming everybody but themselves for their problems, they tend to mix in statements blaming others with self-blame as well as with self-denigrating or unflattering self-characterizations. If a therapist's interventions imply that that the patient is at fault for a problem, the BPD patient tends to blame others; if the therapist seems to be blaming the others, the BPD patient tends to blame himself or herself. When patients are busy making judgments about who is to blame for a problem, they are less likely to be describing specific interpersonal interactions to the therapist. The therapist counters this tendency through the use of reframing. In the early part of therapy, the therapist validates the patient's observations on which his or her assessment of the blameworthiness of self or others is based, while at the same time subtly challenging the patient's inferences and conclusions based on those observations. Later in therapy, the issue of blame is handled with different techniques that are described shortly.

If a patient blames significant others for his or her problem, the therapist should be careful not to invalidate such comments by pointing out the patient's contributions to the interpersonal difficulty. The patient already knows what they are. Instead, the therapist suggests that perhaps the motivation of the other people is not as bad as their actions might suggest.

When patients with BPD make overly broad self-blaming comments in the context of describing an interpersonal problem, I have found it useful to make the statement, "That's very kind of you to put *all* the blame on yourself for that." This sort of statement rarely draws an argumentative response. It also comes as a surprise to the patient because it is so different from the responses the patient normally gets, and often intrigues the patient.

Another very useful reframing statement used early in therapy with patients with BPD is, "You must have a really good reason for [doing or feeling] that way." This statement is used whenever the patient says something about himself or herself that would usually draw either criticism or argument from others. For example, whenever individuals make global self-deprecating statements such as, "I'm really stupid" while at the same time exhibiting intelligence, the natural tendency of someone hearing them do this is to argue the point. Therapists may, for example, feel an urge to point out all the evidence that argues against the patient's pessimistic self-assessment. With patients with BPD, doing so generally leads to a futile argument. The therapist can instead respond, "You must have a good reason for telling yourself that when it so clearly is not the case."

Usually this therapist intervention is greeted with a sheepish smile from the patient. Occasionally the patient might try to provoke an argument by offering up more concrete examples of how stupid he or she is. When this happens, therapists should refuse to argue by offering up counterexamples; again, the patient already knows what the counterexamples are. The therapist can remain silent or, if pressed, say, "Well that's what I think."

When the patient describes spoiling behavior or clearly self-destructive or dangerous actions, the "good reason" statement should take the form, "You must have a really good reason for doing that when it's so obviously [painful or counterproductive] for you. You obviously are not enjoying it, and I do not believe in masochism." This statement is another surprise for BPD patients. Someone in authority is telling them that they must have a good reason for their actions! Usually they are told that they are some kind of idiot when they talk or behave that way.

The patient's response to this reframing statement usually ranges from the aforementioned sheepish smile to a half-hearted argument that, if the therapist really thinks that the patient has a good reason for the behavior in question, the therapist must not have been listening very carefully. The therapist again should refuse to argue the point. Alternately, the patient may ask, "What on earth could be a good reason for doing *that?*" Therapists should reply that they do not know yet, but that finding the answer to this question is a very important task on which the patient and therapist should work. This might also be a good time to ask the Adlerian question, which is described shortly.

Yet another type of criticism-drawing statement made frequently by patients with BPD, particularly females, occurs when a therapist inquires as to why a patient is remaining in an abusive relationship. The typical response is, "Because I love him!" or, in the case of parents, "Because they're my parents!" Therapists who hear this answer may be overcome with a mixture of feelings of helplessness and fury. They may experience an urge to yell back, "How can you love someone who acts like that? What's the matter with you?" or, "So what if they are your parents!"

I find it useful to reframe love as a positive emotion. The "love" often is related to the fact that, because of the patient's family dynamics, an abusive spouse is meeting some ambivalently experienced need by the patient to be with an abusive spouse. Affinity toward one's parents, on the other hand, is programmed into our very souls. My usual intervention is to beat the patient to the punch by saying, "You must really love him [them] a lot to put up with that kind of treatment!"

Reverse Free Association. If the therapist has retained empathy with and has showed genuine interest and regard for the patient with BPD, and has validated the patient as much as possible while responding well to provocative behavior, the patient will usually begin to trust the therapist. This usually takes a minimum of seven or eight sessions. At this point, the therapist can become more overt about zeroing in on family-of-origin interactions as the most likely factor in maintaining the patient's problem behavior and symptoms. The therapist begins to point out to the patient possible parallels between any relationship episodes that the patient is reporting during the session and important family interactions that have been described previously.

In order to discern potential analogies and parallels between the stories patients tell and their family-of-origin experience, the therapist can make use of his or her own subconscious. The human brain tends to incorporate data into memory through a process of automatically comparing a newly perceived entity with similar entities perceived or known previously (Edelman, 1989). In doing psychotherapy, I attempt to harness this brain mechanism through a process that I refer to as *reverse free association*. As the patient describes a relationship episode or even a dream, I let my mind wander to anything else I already know about the patient. I might suddenly recall something the patient told me in the social history that was obtained during the patient's initial evaluation, or a relationship episode the patient described in an earlier session. The recalled item usually pops into my mind precisely because of some similarity to the data being provided in the current session. Reviewing one's notes on the client just prior to a therapy session is a good way to prime the brain for this sort of activity.

In other words, therapists can free associate to whatever the patient is telling them. However, they do not associate to things in their *own* life that might occur to them; they associate to other things in the *patient's* life. To use this technique, therapists ask themselves, "What else in the patient's life does this make me think of?" and then let their minds wander.

When the therapist first notices that the patient is describing interpersonal difficulties that seem to be or might possibly be analogous to family-of-origin behavior or issues, the therapist can make a statement such as "When you told me about that argument you had with your boss, it reminded me of what you told me about you and your father."

After making such an observation, the therapist should make no further comment, but expectantly wait for a reaction. The therapist should hear what the patient has to say about the observation before drawing any conclusions. Otherwise, the therapist might prematurely endorse a parallel that may not exist, may be only partially accurate, or is one that the patient may not be quite ready to endorse. Later in therapy, if the therapist has stronger data on which to draw parallels, he or she can make a more definitive statement on the matter, although even then it is best to do so somewhat tentatively.

Patients in therapy often spontaneously describe dreams, sometimes because of previous therapy with a psychodynamically oriented therapist. Rather than asking the patient to associate to the dream and its elements as an analyst might do, the therapist can instead use reverse free association. Rather than offering a dream interpretation, therapists tells the patient which family-of-origin issues the dream makes them think of, and then await a response from the patient. If no links are apparent, the therapist can say that he or she is not sure what the dream might refer to, and listen for further information that may later shed light on it.

A good example of a therapist's use of reverse free association occurred in the psychotherapy of a young woman (Case 8-A) who had dropped out of college several times. She was not sure why she seemed unable to finish school; she reported that after a while she just could not seem to "handle the stress." She liked the idea of being an intellectual, but found herself drawn to the uneducated. She referred to the latter as *low lifes.* As she described these conflicts, the therapist suddenly recalled something the patient had said in the course of providing her social history during her initial evaluation. The mother had reportedly used the term *low life* to describe the patient's father, with whom the mother had had a one night stand that had resulted in the birth of the patient.

The therapist said, "When you said 'low life' it reminded me of what you said about how your mother described your father." Without further prompting, the patient then recalled that the mother had been the black sheep in her own family of origin. She, too, had wanted to go to college but had never been quite able to make it happen. It later turned out that the patient felt pressure to follow in her mother's footsteps, so to speak.

Relating Marital Problems to Family of Origin Issues.   If the patient's complaints center on marital issues, the therapist also looks for ties to family-of-origin issues. The therapist should ask patients about the reactions of parents and in-laws to their marital difficulties. In BPD patients, family responses often includes such reactions as negative comments about the spouse or patient, confusing or contradictory demands about how to handle the marital conflict, or seeming parental envy of the patient's marriage. As data is gathered, the therapist attempts to demonstrate how and why the family-of-origin issues make resolution of the marital difficulties far more difficult than they might be otherwise. Establishing the relevance of the family of origin to marital issues may also involve the use of the three other techniques that I now describe: the Adlerian question, focusing on mixed messages from the family of origin, and focusing on ambivalent expectations and cross-motive reading within the marital relationship.

The Adlerian Question.   The psychoanalytic pioneer Alfred Adler was the first to advocate asking patients about what negative consequences might ensue if somehow by magic the problems they presented with were completely solved (Mosak, 1989). This question or variations of it have been adopted by several different psychotherapies, including family systems therapy, solution-oriented therapy (the "miracle question," [De Shazer, 1988]), and brief therapy (Gustafson, 1986). The posing of this question in the early part of therapy is an essential component of unified therapy with patients with BPD. The question is designed to trace the adverse consequences within the patient's family of origin that might occur should the patient stop self-destructive, self-defeating, or spoiling behavior patterns.

To almost all problems, there is a conventional solution that seems obvious—so obvious in fact that the therapist should assume that the patient has already thought of it. Presentation by the therapist of such a "solution" to a BPD patient invariably leads to a game of "why don't you—yes but" (Berne, 1964). The therapist should instead pose the Adlerian question, "If I could magically make this problem go away, what would be the downside?" Examples are: "If somehow you could get over your fear of asking nice women out, what additional problems would that create?" and "Everyone is probably advising you to tell your father that your affairs are none of his business. I wonder if something bad would happen if you did that." The therapist then listens for a possible and likely adverse consequence that in most cases entails some sort of extreme and frightening negative response from important family members.

If the patient is confused by the question, the therapist might ask the patient to visualize having successfully overcome the problem and then ask, "What's wrong with this picture?" Alternatively, the therapist may ask the patient directly who might be affected negatively if the patient were better adjusted.

The therapist should not accept as a complete response an answer that, should the problem be solved, the patient would merely find some other way to unsolve it. Patients might tell the therapist, for instance, that the negative consequences of solving the problem would be an alteration or escalation of their self-destructive or self-defeating behavior. An example is "If I got up the nerve to ask a nice girl for a date, I would probably end up making a fool of myself over dinner." All this means is that the patient, if deprived of his or her usual ways of playing out a family role, would merely find another way to act it out. It avoids the question of why the patient is playing the role in the first place. In such a case, the therapist should go a step further and ask the patient what would happen if he or she were successful in his or her *ultimate* goal. In the just-mentioned example, the therapist would ask, "What would be the downside if you were able to have a totally successful relationship with a nice woman?"

Another type of incomplete answer is a reply that the negative consequence of solving the presenting problem would solely be some manifestation of existential anxiety. An example of this type of answer is "If I started dating really nice women, I'd start picking at my skin until I bled." Again, the therapist should go a step further and ask a question about what might be creating the anxiety in the first place. The therapist could say, "Well that just means that you would in fact be very nervous about what your success would mean, but what would that anxiety be about?" Existential fears are also behind such client statements as "That would never happen, so there's no point in thinking about it" or "I can not even visualize being happy like that." The therapist can respond, "So it sounds like, whatever it is, it is too frightening to even contemplate."

In cases in which the negative reaction that the patient fears comes primarily from a spouse or partner, and the patient seems to be avoiding an obvious solution to the couple's problem, this line of inquiry can again be used to find out about the downside of solving that problem. The therapist pursues the issue of who in the patient's family of origin might be affected negatively if the patient were somehow magically able to have a happy marriage.

The Adlerian question may on occasion bring an immediate answer that sheds profound light on the patient's family dilemma. One patient (Case 8-B) told her therapist about how she made herself miserable every day at work by constantly thinking up and worrying about catastrophic occurrences that could take place that day. She did this knowing full well that the scenarios she thought up and feared were extremely unlikely. In fact, they never came to pass. The therapist asked her, "What would happen if you were able to stop yourself from doing that and enjoyed your work?" The patient's immediate response was, "My mother would not know what to do with herself, and she would stop sending me money!"

More often, however, patients at first have difficulty answering the question. They might say, "I can't think of any downside; being rid of my problem would be wonderful." To this, the therapist can reply, "One would certainly think so, but might it create some additional problem for you or somebody else?" If the patient has already described something a family member has said or done in regards to the problem, the therapist might add, "Didn't you tell me your father becomes jealous of you?" If the therapist has nothing to go on, he or she should become silent and wait for the patient to go on. Often times an initial denial that there would be any downside gradually gives way to associations that reveal a significant one.

Eventually, the therapist learns what it is that patients fear might happen to loved ones if they were to, say, stop spoiling behavior. If the therapist has been given an accurate picture, these feared consequences should be plausible, probable, and serious. For example, a patient's mother might get seriously depressed and suicidal, or parents may divorce. It then becomes important for the therapist to discuss and be empathic with the consequences to the patient and his or her family members should the patient give up self-destructive, self-defeating, or misery-producing behavior patterns.

Sometimes patients will respond to the therapist's attempts at empathy in this regard with the proposition that they really do not care what happens to their families, and that their motivation for maladaptive behavior is really selfish. The therapist should then express confusion to the patient about the obvious logical contradiction between self-destructive behavior and selfishness. Some behaviors such as destructive rages or over-eating can be made to look gratifying, but the experience of them, not to mention their consequences, is anything but. The patient is too intelligent to be unaware of this. If the patient continues to argue, the therapist can use the "refusal to argue" technique described in a previous chapter. The only "selfish" motive behind self-destructive behavior that the therapist can agree to is the patient's wish to avoid the anxiety associated with watching his or her family suffer.

If, on the other hand, patients respond to the therapist's intervention by flagellating themselves for being such patsies, the therapist should respond with praise for the client's caring and concern. The therapist can then go on and suggest that perhaps there is a way better than self-sacrifice to express it. The therapist might say, "I think it's great, especially in this day and age, that you are so sensitive to your father's concerns. You are really a caring person. The world needs more of that. Perhaps there's another way to express that concern without destroying yourself in the process." The latter statement alludes to the therapist's intention to offer the patient a way out of his or her dilemma. The way out will be trying to develop understanding and empathy for the behavior of family members in order to discuss family dynamics with them in a way that is palatable for everyone concerned.

When the therapist has successfully focused on the consequences to the patient and his or her family should the patient get better, another common response is for the patient to gradually become outraged at the family for creating this situation. The patient may in anger begin to attribute evil motives for the behavior to significant family members. Although this anger may certainly be justified and should not be invalidated, the solution to the patient's problem lies, not with anger at the family, but with empathy. The therapist should respond to this anger with a statement such as, "I don't blame you one bit for being angry; I'm sure I'd feel exactly the same way. However, perhaps we can find a way to look at your family's behavior that makes it more understandable."

Whenever the patient begins to blame the misbehavior of family members on their being malevolent, crazy, or mentally retarded, the therapist can suggest that perhaps the others are actually reacting badly because of their own internal conflicts and sensitivities. The therapist may bring up any information, previously shared by the patient, that indicates that the family member in question really does care about the patient or can act intelligently. This intervention sets the stage for a later intervention: giving a rationale for gathering genogram material that might put the family misbehavior in a more understandable light.

Focusing on Ambivalence in and Mixed Messages From the Patient and Family Members.   After identifying family behavior that triggers the patient's difficulties, an important step in making the family behavior more comprehensible to the patient is identifying the family members' internal conflicts. The therapist should use questions that focus on each important family member's communication and behavior patterns, as reported by the patient in therapy, that might indicate ambivalence and confusion over various role functions and mutual expectations. An important indicator that such a question is in order is when patients or members of their family are described as exhibiting oppositional, distancing, or ambiguous behavior with one another.

Often patients describe what they believe to be their parents' expectations of them, based on what the parents are saying to them, while seeming to ignore evidence from the context of the relationship that contradicts the parents' verbal requests. A common pattern that illustrates this phenomenon was observed in the therapy of a middle-aged man (8-C) who believed that his elderly widowed mother was too dependent on him. She incessantly demanded that he wait on her hand and foot. However, she always demanded that he come over to help her at times clearly inconvenient for him—as if he had nothing else to do—and criticized him relentlessly for not coming around more often. The therapist remarked, "I'm sure your mother is an intelligent woman. She has to notice that her demands annoy you and feed into your resolve to refuse her requests."

In response to this intervention, the patient countered that the mother really was too stupid to appreciate that such requests might backfire. In similar cases, other patients might instead have suggested that she was too hostile to care or too crazy to know. The therapist responded, "I don't know, she seems to be quite bright from the way you describe her. I bet she knows." The patient still disagreed; the therapist did not argue but listened for further evidence of the mother's intelligence. As the evidence mounted the therapist then said, "I know you said you thought your mother wasn't very bright, but she was able to do [list of examples]. That makes me think she's brighter than she has led you to believe."

Interestingly, when I have suggested to patients that they might be harboring a negative image of a parent, they have in many cases brought up contradictory evidence themselves. For example, in cases such as 8-C in which patients have gone on and on about how often their mothers demand attention, I have said, "You must think she does not want you to have your own life so you can wait on her hand and foot!" In response, some patients have wanted to argue about this and have made statements such as, "Yeah, but she really resents it when I try to do too much for her," or "Well, yeah, but she always criticizes herself for taking up so much of my time."

Such patients are not trying to be contrary; in fact, in the previously discussed cases the patients' and therapists' statements were both true. The mothers in these cases were undoubtedly ambivalent about having their sons help them. Unified therapy generally looks for "both–and" explanations rather than "either–or" ones. The therapist can agree with patients who point out examples of when a parent acts in a manner opposite to the usual way, and ask them how they reconcile the parent's apparently contradictory behavior. Alternatively, the therapist can be empathic with how confusing the parent's behavior must be.

Focusing on Cross-Motive Reading. The therapist should attempt to clarify what happens when various family members try to guess one another's intentions and motives simultaneously, especially in those situations where ambivalence and mixed messages reign. The goal here is to demonstrate to patients that both they and the relative are grappling with the same issues. The patients can then better understand the relative's strange behavior by comparing the family member's dilemma to their own confusion. The therapist tries to show the patient how cross-motive reading leads to incorrect or incomplete assessments of the motives of family members.

To illustrate, let us continue with the type of situation exemplified by 8-C. After the therapist has clarified that the patient is getting a double message from the mother about her needing the patient to be "on call" for her, the therapist might then suggest that perhaps the mother is also misunderstanding the patient. In response to the confusing signals from the mother, the patient may be unknowingly giving out a double message himself. He may complain vociferously, for example, about the mother's requests for help and how annoying they are, yet continuously cancel his other activities in order to fulfil the mother's every demand. In Case 8-C, the therapist noted that the patient had had no stable long-term romantic relationships, and wondered aloud, "Perhaps your mother is misreading your attentiveness. It is possible that she incorrectly thinks you are using her needs as an excuse for avoiding other relationships, or something like that."

The goal of this intervention was to put the mother's unreasonable-appearing behavior in a more positive light, so that the patient could gain an empathic perspective. If the intervention has worked well, the patient then considers the possibility that he is feeding into the problem with his own behavior. How the therapist phrases the intervention is quite important; the therapist does not want to appear to be blaming the patient for his mother's neurotic activities. It is important to emphasize very clearly that the mother may be reading the patient *incorrectly* or that the patient is feeding into the problem *inadvertently*.

If the Patient's Material Is Not Leading Anywhere, Offer Hypotheses. This technique is used in those sessions in which the therapist's attempts to get clarification about family patterns from the patient result in any of the following:

1. The patient is consistently quiet or withdrawn.
2. The patient repeats the same stories over and over again without lending any deepening to the therapist's understanding of the patient's family dynamics.
3. The patient seems to be making idle chit chat that does not address central concerns or family issues.

In these instances, the therapist might first make a process comment noting how the patient is acting and then express concern about it. If that fails to get the patient to open up, another useful technique is for the therapist to offer the patient speculations about family interpersonal processes that may be triggering problematic feelings or behavior. There is something about tentatively offering patients a hypothesis that makes it difficult for them to merely agree or disagree. Hypotheses seem to demand more from patients than questions; they increase the likelihood that the patient will feel it necessary to tell the therapist what is wrong or right with the hypothesis, rather than just giving the therapist an unexplained acceptance or rejection of it. This is especially true if the therapist overtly labels the intervention as a guess, thereby giving patients an out that allows them to reject the guess. This technique makes it difficult for the patient to get into a power struggle with the therapist over the accuracy of the hypothesis.

The therapist can base speculations or hypotheses on any information concerning the patient and his or her family that is already available, or on typical patterns that the therapist has seen or read about in other patients with similar problems. Such suggestions should always be made in a tentative and nonthreatening manner. For example, the therapist might say something like, "I don't know if this applies to you or not, but in other families where a woman's career choice is an issue, mothers often seem jealous of their daughters because the daughter gets to do things the mother was not free to do. I wonder if this might apply to your situation?"

Provision of a Rationale for the Interpersonal, Family-of-Origin Focus. At some point during therapy, therapists should explain to the patient explicitly why they are focusing on family relationship issues. This is usually done after they have collected enough information from the patient to make a case for a strong relationship between the patient's family's behavior and his or her current symptomatology, dysfunctional relationship patterns, or self-destructive acting out. Therapists should try to impart to the patient that the family-relationship patterns, as manifested by specific family verbalizations or behavior, feed into the patient's difficulties. Therapists should be alert to, and attempt to counter, patient resistance to the interpersonal focus; they should never ignore a patient's reservations about that focus.

One type of evidence that is particularly helpful in convincing the patient that the therapist's focus is the best one is a patient report that he or she had a strong emotional reaction—similar to his or her presenting symptom—after an interaction with a parent. For example, one patient (Case 8-D) with the chief complaint of anxiety belatedly told me that she became nauseous after each and every daily conversation with her mother. I pointed out that this reaction most likely meant that her interactions with her mother were a major determinant of her emotional problems.

Sometimes patients question the therapist's family focus before the therapist has enough information to make a strong case for its centrality. If this should happen, the therapist can tell the patient that such issues are the primary difficulty for many patients who have similar problems. In addition, the therapist can list whatever minimal evidence is available that the patient may be in a similar position, and state that this list is suggestive that the therapist's line of inquiry will eventually yield fruit.

The therapist can also indicate an open-minded attitude toward competing explanations by inviting the patient to come up with a different hypothesis about the reasons for maladaptive behavior or symptoms. In response, the patient may offer a competing hypothesis that is illogical or overly pat. If the patient offers a competing hypothesis that seems to be unreasonable, the therapist should tactfully express puzzlement over any apparent inconsistencies or logical fallacies.

If the patient's explanation seems too pat or incomplete, the therapist can respond by tactfully suggesting that, although the patient's explanation may be partially correct, there must be more to it. A common example of a pat explanation is the "single traumatic event hypothesis." Examples are "My continuing depression over the last 20 years stemmed from being fondled one time by the teenager next door when I was 6," or "My anxiety about going to school was caused by the 7th-grade English teacher who humiliated me in front of the class." In my opinion, the effects of most single traumatic events are insufficiently powerful to explain the severity and pervasiveness of a BPD patient's ongoing problems. The vast majority of individuals exposed to such a trauma get over it. The fact that the patient did not get over it usually indicates family involvement in the problem that is unacknowledged. The therapist might then ask about the family's reaction to the event, or about what else was going on in the patient's life at that time.

Gathering Genogram Data.   As the patient and therapist focus on the confusing and contradictory nature of the behavior of the patient's family members, the question of why they act that way naturally arises. This question sets the stage for the gathering of genogram information. The therapist uses genogram information from at least three generations to clarify for the patient the origins of and the reasons for the family's dysfunctional behavior patterns. The unified therapist may and should ask about extended family members and their past and current behavior, conflicts, and reactions whenever possible, no matter the stage of therapy, especially if the patient brings them up. However, after the therapist has gathered extensive data about the patient's interactions with family-of-origin members, and if the therapist has not already done so, the rationale behnind such questions should be described explicitly.

The therapist informs the patient that a strategy for altering destructive interpersonal patterns can best be worked out if the patient and therapist can figure out the nature and causes of negative family member reactions. This, in turn, can best be accomplished through examining the background of the family members in question. The therapist then actively and persistently pursues information that helps to clarify the patient's family dynamics, with the ultimate goal of helping the patient to become empathic with important family members. The therapist gathers such information by employing direct questioning, follow-up questions, and the technique of hypothesizing about possible interrelationships.

The therapist looks for parallels and similarities between the interactions of the patient with his or her family-of-origin members and other past or present interactions within the extended family. In particular, the therapist needs to know details about the relationships between the patient's parents and grandparents, both at present and during the parents' childhood, as well as about the relationship of the grandparents with one another. The therapist also needs to know about major cultural or historical events that have impacted the family, such as immigration to a new and alien culture, sudden deaths, or changes in family status. Although it is often not possible to trace family conflicts back to the time before the birth of the parents, if such information is available, it too should be sought out actively.

If the client does not know much about what family relationships were like in earlier times and generations, the patient should be advised to seek out collateral sources of information, and coached on how to make use of them. The therapist encourages patients to consult any available sources, including older relatives, the parents themselves, existing family trees or histories, or old newspaper articles. Unfortunately, traditional genealogical sources such as immigration records or county records rarely give usable information regarding family relationship patterns, so their use should not be encouraged. If living family members are loathe to provide genogram information, or if the patient thinks that they would react negatively if asked, the therapist employs role-playing techniques to coach the patient on how to extract information from them. These techniques, which are the same as those used for several other purposes, are described in detail in the next chapter.

OFFERING THE SOLUTION

In this section, I outline the procedure for setting the stage for the most important part of therapy: coaching the patient on how to get past the family's formidable defenses in order to effectively metacommunicate with them about the family behavior patterns that are causing trouble for the patient. This is accomplished by the presentation of a hypothesis or interpretation about the main family issues and by outlining for the patient a strategy for change.

Hypothesis Presentation.   After the therapist has gathered enough data about current family interrelationship patterns and about their historical genesis, he or she attempts to fashion a preliminary hypothesis regarding the genesis and maintenance of the patient's self-destructive behavior and symptoms. For patients with BPD, the hypothesis will almost invariably center on the reasons for, manifestations of, and the patient's reaction to the parents' ambivalence toward the patient, as discussed in Part I. The therapist then provides the patient with a tentative interpretation about the reasons for the problematic family patterns that reinforce the patient's dysfunctional behavior or symptomatology. Hypothesis presentation sets the stage for offering a solution for the patient's core problems. If there is more than one significant issue, there may be more than one interpretation. If there are two or more core conflictual themes, the therapist should spell out which issues are central and salient and which are secondary and less salient.

Interpretations are always presented as hypotheses, not as facts. The therapist can easily be mistaken about parts of them, or an entire hypothesis may be off track. After hearing an interpretation, the patient may bring up information not divulged previously that may necessitate alteration of the hypothesis. Ultimately, the reactions and comments of the patient's whole family during metacommunication will verify or refute the approximate truth of the hypothesis.

I use the word *approximate* here for two reasons. First, as with all human knowledge, any explanation the therapist may offer is only an approximation of reality. Reality can never be completely known. More important, no hypothesis will account for *all* of the known data. No matter how well crafted, the hypothesis will almost always have some loose ends or inconsistencies. It is not essential for the therapist to tie up everything in a nice neat package. The hypothesis need only be a close approximation to the essence of the family struggle.

During hypothesis presentation, the therapist first reviews and clarifies the interrelationship patterns and cross-motive reading, elucidated earlier in therapy, that reinforce the patient's difficulties. Second, the therapist makes an informed guess about why family members behave as they do based on the genogram information previously obtained. Last, the therapist informs the patient that the hypothesis about the other family members is tentative and subject to direct confirmation from the involved relatives.

After the therapist has presented the hypothesis and the patient has at least partially accepted it, the issue of "who is to blame" often arises once again. Once again, the therapist should attempt to replace the patient's impulse to blame someone with the ideas of shared personal responsibility and empathy for others. The therapist can make two points in this regard. First, the patient was not forced, but volunteered to make sacrifices because of his or her care and concern. Although they may have had no choice as children, at some point in their adult lives patients gained the ability to accept or reject the family "script." Second, the whole family shares the whole problem. Everyone is responding to his or her own conflicts. The therapist should, if possible, describe any commonalties between the experiences and conflicts of the patient and those of the blamed relative.

Another issue that may come up after hypothesis presentation is manifested when patients begin to flagellate themselves for not understanding the family's behavior better prior to therapy. The therapist can reassure them by making two points. First, in the past the patient had no way of knowing the real reasons for the behavior of other family members. The therapist was able to figure it out, with the patient's help, only because of his or her many years of studying the intricacies of human behavior. Second, the conclusions that the patient *did* reach, although partially incorrect, were in fact logical and based on the evidence at hand.

Presentation of an Outline for the Solution to the Problem and Provision of a Rationale for It. The therapist next presents to the patient the idea that the solution to the problem rests with empathic metacommunication. The therapist informs the patient that significant others who feed into the patient's problem behavior and symptoms can be confronted in a way that will get them to stop doing that. If this process is successful, the patient will then feel freer to behave differently and will feel better.

The therapist also makes the following points: First, any problem must be discussed openly in order to be solved. Second, the behavior within the relationship between the patient and that family member *must* change if the patient changes his or her approach. The other person is literally forced to respond differently. Third, the patient is not responsible for changing the behavior of family members with anybody else. Nonetheless, it is possible that the patient's efforts may be quite helpful to the confronted family member in ways that transcend their immediate relationship. There is no guarantee that it will be, but the effort to discuss family dynamics will most certainly be far more helpful to the targeted others than the sacrifices the patient already is and has been making for them.

The initial reaction of patients with BPD to the suggestion that they should talk about difficult behavior patterns with their parents is fairly predictable. The patient will look at the therapist as if the therapist has completely lost his or her mind. The patient will then come up with arguments against proceeding with the therapist's advice. The arguments are almost always variations on the twin themes of, "You do not *know* how impossible my family is" and "I'm just not capable of doing that."

Patients who say these things are not trying to give the therapist a hard time, nor are they questioning his or her expertise. They are merely reacting to their own extensive experience. In the families of BPD patients, attempts at holding such conversations almost invariably lead to disaster; perhaps the therapist just does not quite understand how invalidating the parents can be. In response, the therapist needs to help the patient understand that, by altering the patient's approach to family members through a process of tailoring statements to family sensitivities, such conversations can be successfully negotiated.

The patient's concerns must all be addressed; a list of typical concerns and suggestions for how the therapist can address them follows shortly. If, after these concerns are addressed, the patient remains skeptical but is willing to try out role-playing potential strategies to see what the therapist can come up with—the next step in psychotherapy—the therapist may proceed despite the skepticism. If the patient remains unconvinced that *any* way around the family's defenses exists, the therapist suggests that the patient allow the therapist to at least try to come up with one, so the patient can see what it is before deciding whether or not to actually implement the therapist's plan. The therapist then reassures patients that they will not be asked to do anything that they believe can not work.

The following are five objections that the patient might have to the proposed solution, and suggestions for how the therapist can handle them:

1. "My family members can not handle such an emotionally difficult discussion." Counters: The therapist, while praising the patient for his or her desire to protect relatives from unpleasant feelings, makes the point that people are stronger than they may appear. In fact, protecting family members actually makes them appear to be more fragile than they actually are. For example, if everyone in the family is walking on eggshells around Mom out of a fear that she might be fragile, she is bound to notice. In response, she will begin to doubt herself. After all, if everyone else thinks she is weak, perhaps she really is. In other words, individuals tend to overreact precisely because everyone around them has been feeding into their sense of fragility. Second, abstaining from problem-solving discussions in order

to avoid unpleasant feelings backfires. Doing so prevents the family from resolving issues and eventually feeling better. Although family members may temporarily experience an exacerbation of depression or anxiety when confronted with their own conflicts, they are already feeling those feelings anyway, regardless of whether the patient brings up troublesome issues or not.

2. "My family would never be amenable to such a discussion no matter how I approach them." Patients frequently believe that their family is more difficult to talk to than any other family in existence or that all possible approaches have already been tried and have failed. Counter: The therapist reassures the patient that the therapist is confident that approaches that work with even the most dysfunctional of families can be designed. Perhaps there might be some tactics of which the patient is unaware. If the patient still refuses to work on family metacommunication, the therapist can, as mentioned previously, ask the patient to reserve judgment on proceeding until after the patient and therapist have had a chance to complete the role-playing exercises.

3. "I want nothing to do with my family; they are just too awful." The patient may say this even after complaining for months, in so many words, about how he or she is enmeshed with the family. Counter: The therapist points out that, judging from the extent of the patient's reactions, the family still generates strong feelings in the patient even if contact is minimal. Such strong feelings indicate that the patient still cares about them regardless of what they have done. The therapist may also point out that the patient really would want a relationship with them if they stopped their aggravating behavior. Such a change is exactly what the therapist is attempting to bring about.

4. "The prospect of bring up touchy issues is just too terrifying." Counter: The therapist tells patients that most people find the prospect of confronting touchy issues with their family frightening, and that this feeling is perfectly normal, understandable, and predictable. However, while being empathic with the extent of the patient's feelings, the therapist does not want to reinforce the patient's belief that the fear is unbearable. He or she can reassure the patient that the hardest step is getting

started, but that the process usually gets considerably easier as it goes along.

5. "I shouldn't be the one that has to do this; they should take care of this themselves." The patient complains of the unfairness of the whole procedure. After all, the parents had the problem first; why should solving it fall to the patient? Counter: The therapist is empathic with the fact that this is unfair, but points out that the patient's sacrifice indicates that he or she already *is* taking responsibility for the family problem. Unfair or not, the patient was the one to come for help, and is now the only one with the understanding of the family dynamics necessary in order to do the job.

In the next section, we look at what the therapist should do if the patient wants to invite family members or a spouse in for a conjoint session. Requests from the patient for a conjoint session may come at any time during therapy, and the unified therapist should, except at the very start of therapy, agree to them in most instances.

CONJOINT SESSIONS

Conjoint sessions with the patient and one other relative can speed up the process of therapy in a number of ways. Therapists can use a conjoint session to confirm their impressions about a family member or about family dynamics, gather additional relational and genogram data, and facilitate the process of family metacommunication.

Patients request conjoint sessions for many of these same reasons. They may want to have the therapist get additional information that they have not been able to get, show the therapist what problematic reactions they are up against, or have the therapist help them tell other family members about the family issues identified in therapy. However, patients may also want the therapist to directly mediate disputes; that request should be denied. If the therapist does the task for patients, they would never learn how to do it themselves. The therapist is not going to be around all the time, and it is a relative certainty that the problematic family behavior will recur from time to time even after a successful intervention. Nonetheless, if the metacommunication process is stuck, one or two conjoint sessions with a given relative or spouse may be useful; such sessions can be used to get the ball rolling again or to help speed up the patient's learning process.

If patients request that more than one relative come to a session together, the therapist should advise them that it is best if relatives come in one at a time. Inviting the whole family in is disadvantageous in families of patients with BPD for two reasons. First, behavior in BPD families can quickly escalate into vicious mutual invalidation or even violence; the more people present, the more difficult it is for anyone to control the proceedings. This is the reason that, later in therapy, the patient is taught to confront family members one at a time. Second, having the whole family come makes the session look too much like family therapy. The conjoint session, as will be described shortly, is framed as something else.

Successful conjoint sessions require advanced planning. The therapist adheres to the following procedures when the patient requests a conjoint session: First, the therapist tells the patient that, in order to be most helpful, the therapist needs to be free, as the need arises, to bring up any information that the he or she already knows. Permission to do so is requested and obtained from the patient so that confidentiality is not an issue. Patients who refuse this permission are warned that the conjoint sessions will probably not be of much help. The therapist may agree, however, not to bring up certain items specified by the patient in advance such as an extramarital affair. In such cases the therapist should nonetheless insist on being free to bring up the issues that may have led to the affair.

Second, the therapist informs the patient about how the therapist plans to conduct the conjoint session. The therapist says that he or she plans to start the session by asking for the relative's opinion about the *patient's* problems. The therapist then adds that doing so does not imply that the therapist believes that any interpersonal problem is the fault of the patient alone.

The rationale for the approach is then given to the patient explicitly. The approach serves two purposes. First, the relative is apt to anticipate that the patient and therapist, having already formed a relationship, will gang up against him or her. Therapists are notorious for blaming all of their patient's ills on parents. The parents of patients with BPD in particular are exquisitely sensitive to anything that suggests that they have not been exemplary. Their extreme defensiveness is a shield for their unexpressed guilt and shame; secretly they are terrified that they have been terrible parents. They worry that their child hates them, especially if they had been abusive. When invited to a psychotherapy session, they expect bad things to happen.

In some cases bad things may have already happened to them with the patient's previous therapist. For example, the parents of one patient (Case 8-E) were ambushed in an initial conjoint session by a previous therapist with the news that the patient's older brother had, as a teen, molested her. Before the session was through, however, the parents had convinced the therapist that the patient was outrageously exaggerating what had been innocuous and innocent horseplay. The likelihood that this patient and her parents would ever again agree to meet together with a therapist was minuscule.

Instead of confronting parents with bad news or accusations, the unified therapist surprises them by treating them like respected consultants. Doing so communicates to the parents that the therapist has empathy for them and considers their opinions to be valuable. This approach is often very reassuring to a parent, gets the session off to a peaceful start, and leads to a fruitful one.

The therapist tells the patient that the approach of asking the relative's opinion about the patient's problems will make the relative more comfortable and therefore make it more likely that he or she will open up. The therapist then tells the patient the second reason for the recommended approach: The therapist really does want to hear the relative's opinion about the patient. The relative's opinions will help the therapist understand that person's thought processes, and help clarify how he or she reads the motives of the patient. The relative's opinion's may also—although this part is not necessarily stated to the patient explicitly—provide the therapist with invaluable information about mixed messages and cross-motive reading within the patient's family.

If the patient agrees to the recommended protocol, the patient is then instructed to invite the relative to come to a session. The patient is told to be honest with the relative if asked the reason for the invitation: The therapist is interested in how the relative views the patient's difficulties.

Conducting Conjoint Sessions. The therapist starts the conjoint session by greeting the relative warmly and proceeding with the agreed-on intervention. He or she then listens attentively to what the relative's pet theories are about the patient, and coaxes the family member to be frank. As the session develops, the therapist boldly brings up any relevant issue or question, known from earlier sessions, that the patient and family member clearly seem to be avoiding. These issues may include, depending on the stage of therapy:

1. Dyadic interactions from the past that bear on a current misunderstanding within the dyad.
2. Issues in therapy on which the relative should have been informed but has not been.
3. Questions about family history the patient has been afraid to ask.
4. Patient thoughts and feelings previously expressed to the therapist, but about which the patient is being vague or ambiguous in the conjoint session.

The therapist should bring up these issues in a matter-of-fact way, and then immediately sit back and listen without much additional comment. In effect, the issues are thrown back to the dyad. The reason for doing so is that the therapist is not there to be a family counselor per se, but to facilitate the process by which family members themselves must learn to interact. The therapist brings up taboo or touchy issues and watches how the interaction develops, noting both the strengths and weaknesses in the ways that the members of the dyad typically metacommunicate.

If the session has been set up well, patients and family members are usually on their best behavior. They may be quite reluctant to say anything that the other person might find offensive, or conversely, they may be more open about themselves and the family history than they ever have been before. On the other hand, there are instances when patients and family members exhibit their worst behavior, with no apparent shame, right in front of the therapist. They may begin to attack each other unmercifully. Should this happen, the therapist should immediately change course. He or she should try to stop these potentially dangerous interactions by speaking to each party separately, each in the presence of the other. If the patient or the family member speaks out of turn, the therapist asks that such comments be kept for later so that both of them can have their say. If the family member, when invited to speak, continues to attack or viciously invalidate the patient—or vice versa—the therapist should interrupt with a comment that such verbalizations are likely to be counterproductive.

If the therapist is unable to stop the members of the dyad from verbally ripping one another to shreds, it is probably best to stop the session quickly before things get out of hand. The therapist can get up and thank the invited relative for coming in, and indicate that the therapy session should now proceed with the patient alone. When once again alone with the patient, the therapist can express empathy for what the patient has had to face, as evidenced by the preceding interaction, but nonetheless express optimism that a strategy for improving the relationship can still be devised.

When a more successful conjoint session is over, the therapist thanks the relative profusely for coming to the session, and adds that the relative's input has been a great help. If there are issues remaining that were not covered, the relative can be invited back for one additional session. If possible, it is sometimes also helpful for the therapist to remark that, despite any tension between the patient and the relative, he or she can see that they really do care about one another.

In the next chapter, we look at how to plan and implement strategies for the initiation and continuation of family metacommunication so that the patient and the family can have a calm, nondefensive, non attacking, nonblaming and well-reasoned conversation about problematic family patterns.

9

Strategies for Problem Resolution

The therapist uses a role-playing process with patients to devise and teach metacommunicative strategies, tailored individually to each patient's family for solving the patient's difficulties. Role playing is used to develop and practice strategies for extracting genogram information from a reluctant relative, detriangulating peripheral relatives who might interfere with metacommunication with parental figures, and solving core relationship problems through metacommunication with the key family players. Role playing techniques help the patient and therapist accurately anticipate possible negative reactions from various family members and figure out strategies for preventing them.

The ultimate goal for the patient is to request from targeted relatives specific changes in those behaviors and communication patterns that trigger or feed into the patient's self-destructive or self-defeating behavior. The patient's job is not to "fix" the parents in any sense, but only to permanently alter his or her own interactions with them. Nonetheless, if anything will help the parents confront core problems in their own lives and in their other relationships, a discussion of the genesis and manifestations of role function ambivalence within the family system will do so. Altering the targeted family member's behavior with other people, however, is not the patient's responsibility.

Patients must discuss in some detail their own dysfunctional relationship patterns with each relative—usually parental figures—who plays a major part in reinforcing their self-destructive or self-defeating behavior. All primary issues and secondary issues that play into these patterns must eventually be covered with each of these relatives. For patients with BPD, primary issues almost always concern the parental figures' ambivalence about having children and its manifestations and effects on the patient, as well as parental behavior or comments that have had the effect of invalidating the patient. Secondary issues generally involve those family patterns discussed in Part I that reinforce comorbid personality disorder features.

The patients' overall therapeutic task involves a number of component tasks. For each issue with each targeted relative, patients will need to communicate an empathic understanding of the context of the target's difficult behavior, and acknowledge their own contribution to the problem, if any. This discussion of the context of the problem will, in most cases, involve explaining to the target the patient's understanding of the family history and dynamics that created the context. In a sense, patients in therapy are coached to become unified therapists themselves; they empathically discuss the family dynamics with parental figures in much the same way as the therapist has discussed them with the patients.

The next step in the majority of BPD cases is for patients to bring up, in a highly specific manner, the targeted relative's confusing or mixed messages over key issues. Patients must discuss in concrete behavioral terms how they have in the past interpreted these mixed messages, and what adverse affects the comments and behavior have had on them.

The last thing patients must do for each issue with each relative is to request some specific, concrete behavioral changes in the relationship. Patients may ask the target to do things such as:

1. Become more aware of and be willing to discuss how his or her behavior is affecting them.
2. Refrain from using certain types of inflammatory language.
3. Avoid badgering them to do or not do certain things.
4. Avoid direct interference with their interactions with other relatives, peers, lovers, or employers.

Therapists can obtain a preliminary measurement of the success of a patient's interventions by observing whether or not targeted relatives respond favorably to him or her, or at least alter their usual responses in a positive direction. In successful outcomes, the target usually directly or tacitly confirms some of the patient's ideas about the family dynamics. The ultimate success of the interventions, of course, is measured by concrete improvements in the patient's dysfunctional behavior and symptoms.

In successful outcomes for cases involving physical, sexual, or verbal abuse, the target usually acknowledges, directly or indirectly, that the abuse really took place. Although overt verbal acknowledgment from the abuser is the preferable outcome, he or she need not give it if the abuse is acknowledged tacitly. Tacit acknowledgment is expressed through mechanisms such as not invalidating the patient or denying the abuse after the patient has brought it up. An illustrative case example is provided later in the chapter. Likewise, an overt apology for the abuse is a nice outcome, but the patient must learn to accept as sufficient indirect expressions of regret for what transpired. Patients often want the abusing or distancing target to eat crow, so to speak, for what he or she has done or has been doing. However, insisting on this is counterproductive in the long run. The most important outcome is for the targeted relative to stop the problem behavior, including denial of the abuse, in the present and future. The patient must learn to overcome his or her natural human predilections toward moralistic blaming and seeking revenge.

Last, in a successful outcome the targeted family agrees to try to make the requested behavioral change, or to at least be open to further discussion about it should problematic interactions recur. This agreement should sound reasonably sincere. In general, the patient and the target feel closer to one another after metacommunication has been successfully negotiated. Ultimately, the patient is not required to completely forgive abusive parents, but usually wants to forgive them after ongoing troublesome interactional patterns with them have ceased.

OVERVIEW OF STRATEGY PLANNING

Once the hypothesis about the patient's role in the family dynamics has been presented to the patient and the solution to the problem outlined, the therapist and patient begin to devise strategies for use in meta-communication with the central targets. Central targets are usually parents or stepparents but may include any primary caretakers, role models, or family leaders. The patient will confront one central target at a time. It is often necessary, however, to devise strategies for more than one central target in advance of implementing a strategy with any one of them, because sometimes one target will interfere with the patient's confrontation with another. In such cases, the patient may need to initiate a conversation with one, then stop and initiate a conversation with the other, and go back and forth. It is very important that the patient always talk with each target alone. Otherwise, the targets may get together and gang up on the patient. It is much more difficult to maintain one's poise and successfully implement the strategy in front of *two* disqualifying parents than it is to do it in front of one.

The patient is first asked which parental figure would be easiest to deal with. Strategy planning is started with that relative. Like a good behaviorist, the unified therapist prefers that the patient's first experience with metacommunication be successful. For this reason, the most intractable relatives—and the most intractable issue with each relative—are saved for last.

Before implementing any agreed-on strategy with central targets, however, the therapist must first find out whether any peripheral relatives or friends might interfere with the patient's efforts. In most families, someone invariably catches wind of the patient's intentions to bring up touchy issues with parental figures and moves to thwart the effort. This phenomenon is a form of triangulation (Bowen, 1978). Potential triangulators include other central figures, the patient's spouse, siblings, aunts, uncles, grandparents, or even—in unusual cases—close family friends.

The therapist explores with the patient questions about which relatives, if any, might try to subvert the patient's efforts to metacommunicate with salient significant others. The therapist asks pointed, probing questions about various relatives who seem likely to be triangulators. A strategy is then devised for countering any interference from the potential triangulator. Generally, in order to increase the likelihood of success, detriangulating peripheral relatives who might interfere with the implementation of the primary strategy is done prior to actually confronting central targets. Detriangulation strategies are presented later in this chapter.

The patient and therapist begin the development of a strategy for each metacommunicative task through the use of a role-playing process known as role reversal. That is, the patient starts by playing the role of the targeted other while the therapist plays the patient. Role reversal is used anew in strategy planning for each relative who is newly targeted, as well as to begin strategy planning for any new task with relatives who have already been targeted. For example, role reversal is employed again when a therapist who has already worked with the patient on extracting genogram information from a mother goes on to devise a strategy for altering her dysfunctional reactions to the patient. After each role-reversal process is completed, the patient and therapist change places and begin direct role playing. In direct role playing, patients play themselves and practice the newly-devised strategy with the therapist playing the targeted relative.

Role reversal is used to accomplish a number of goals. First, it helps the therapist to experience first hand the kind of family behavior the patient is up against. Often important additional information about either the targeted relative or about the family dynamics surfaces for the first time during role reversal exercises. Second, it allows the therapist to try out different approaches to see which ones are most likely to be successful. Third, it allows the therapist to model promising approaches for the patient. Fourth, it helps the therapist learn how to play the role of the target when the patient practices newly devised strategies in the direct role-playing phase of treatment. Last, through playing the target, the patient often further develops empathy for that person. Patients are forced to put themselves in the shoes of the other person, so to speak, in order to mimic that person.

Although preferable, the patient need not actually get "in character" during role playing. Some patients have great difficulty playing the part of a parent whom they find distasteful. If the patient were to do so, similarities between the patient and the parent might become too obvious for the patient's comfort. Females with BPD, in particular, often hate to be compared to their mothers, or to think of themselves as being anything like their mothers. Nonetheless, the similarities between mother and daughter may be quite striking. In such cases, the patient can still effectively participate in the role-playing process by using the third person when describing how the parent might respond to a strategy the therapist might use. The patient can employ statements such as, "Mom would respond by saying ..."

Before further discussing role reversal and describing specific strategies that the therapist can try out during the process to achieve therapeutic aims, let us first look at some overarching metacommunication strategies that are generally applicable to almost any patient or family.

GENERAL STRATEGIES FOR METACOMMUNICATION

The general principles and techniques described in this section, some of which are mainstays of traditional assertiveness training, may be brought up and taught explicitly to clients in advance of role playing, or they may be taught to clients as the need arises during role playing. If patients demonstrate that they are already aware of some of them, and employ them spontaneously, the therapist need not spell them all out. The therapist should, however, make certain that the patient is aware of them before the patient is told to go out and actually confront a relative in the flesh.

Prior to therapy, attempts by BPD patients to metacommunicate with family members have usually been unsuccessful. Because of everyone's unwillingness to challenge the family homeostasis, motivated by a powerful sense of existential terror, family members have invariably developed a variety of ways to block any of the family's members from discussing taboo subjects. The patient and therapist attempt to devise ways to frustrate the goals of these invalidating behaviors. Instead of causing a stoppage of communication, the target's maneuvers can be used to prolong communication. Instead of leading to distance, the target's maneuvers can be used to move closer. This idea is analogous to the philosophy of judo, in which the offensive moves of antagonists are turned against them. In successful metacommunication, however, both parties come out winners.

The two most important keys to effective metacommunication are maintaining empathy for the target and trying not to protect the target from difficult or unpleasant feelings or realities. At this point in therapy, the patient should already be at least somewhat empathic with misbehaving family members because of the therapist's earlier interventions. Nonetheless, maintaining empathy for someone who has been mistreating you is a very difficult thing to do for any human being, therapists included. Some advice to give to patients to help them do so is described shortly.

In general, the therapist devises ways for the patient to prolong family conversations concerning problematic interpersonal interactions to the point where the initial defenses of the target have fallen away and honest, heartfelt communication takes place. Each conversation should continue to the point at which the patient either reaches an impasse or achieves the goals of the conversation.

Impasses occur when the level of negative emotionality within the dyad starts to increase to the point where the patient feels out of control of it, or when the patient becomes confused and is not sure how to proceed. The therapist tells patients that, should they reach an impasse during a conversation, they should politely back away and tell the target they would like to think more about what has been said. They should then, as soon as possible afterwards while the conversation is still fresh in their minds, write down the conversation as close to verbatim as possible. This includes what they said as well as what the target said. The details of the conversation should then be brought back to the therapist for further strategy planning. If all of the goals for a given conversation with a given relative have been accomplished, the patient should stop the metacommunication process for the time being and go on to other subjects. On some occasions problem resolution can be undone by letting the metacommunication go on for *too* long. In these instances, anger and defensiveness can re-emerge and blaming behavior commence yet again, undoing any previous good feelings.

Let us now briefly review some techniques for reducing emotional overreactivity and maintaining empathy during metacommunication. As the reader will note, these techniques are identical to those that a good therapist uses to reduce transference resistance from a patient.

1. A patient should think of himself or herself as an observer of the interpersonal interaction as well as a participant. The patient gains some emotional distance through the strategy of pretending to watch the interaction as if he or she were a disinterested third party.

2. Before questioning any of a relative's problematic behaviors, patients should first try to find a way to praise the targets' mo-

tivation, or at least give him or her the benefit of the doubt about it.

3. Patients should tactfully verbalize their anger, not attack the target or act the anger out in other ways.

4. When the motives of the significant other are ambiguous, the patient should tactfully verbalize confusion about them.

5. The patient should avoid blaming statements like "You made me do ..." or "You never really cared about me."

6. Patients should make use of disclaimers when describing their reactions to significant others. For example, they might say, "I know you wanted me to be successful, but it often appeared to me that you did not" or "I know you really do care about me but ..."

7. Patients should go back and apologize for any blaming or attacking behavior that might have derailed an earlier attempt at metacommunication. The patients should do so without apologizing for the feelings that led to the earlier misbehavior.

OVERVIEW OF ROLE REVERSAL

The therapist's goal in each role-reversal exercise is to develop a strategy for achieving a specific goal with a targeted relative such as getting genogram information, discussing family dynamics, or directly confronting the significant other with a relationship issue. The therapist tries out different approaches and then shapes a strategy based on the immediate responses that patients demonstrate as they play the role of the targeted relative. The endpoint of the exercise occurs when both the patient and therapist agree that they have devised a strategy that has a high likelihood of success. Of course, the agreed-on strategy, even if performed flawlessly, may still fail when the patient actually confronts the target. Failure at that point means only that the therapist and patient need to figure out what went wrong and why it went wrong, so that they can plan an even better strategy.

The therapist continually modifies strategy during role reversal by using information, generated by the patient while playing the target, about the potential negative and positive reactions of targeted others. The therapist can incorporate information about the target's actual negative responses, and alter the strategy accordingly, when role reversal is being used to redesign a strategy after an initial attempt at in vivo metacommunication has failed or stalemated. Coaching the patient about errors in metacommunication that the patients might *themselves* make is done later during the phase of direct role playing.

Occasionally the therapist's first guess about which strategy might work the best turns out to be correct. If, during role reversal, the patient playing the targeted other reacts favorably to the therapist's strategy right from the start, the therapist may very well be on the right track. In such a case, the therapist can stick with this approach and need not try any others. Most of the time, however, the therapist's initial approach must be continuously modified throughout the role-reversal exercise. Any time the targeted other, as played by the patient, reacts with anger, invalidation of the patient, unusual or frightening behavior, or defensiveness, the therapist knows that the strategy must be further refined. The therapist tries to figure out exactly what was said that the target found threatening, as well as why it was threatening. Might he or she be feeling attacked, blamed, unappreciated, or misunderstood? If so, in precisely what way and for what? A thorough understanding of the family dynamics is useful for understanding how the therapist, while playing the role of the patient, might have offended the targeted other.

As an example of the kind of problem the therapist tries to anticipate and prevent, let us look at an unsuccessful attempt at metacommunication. It took place in the previously described case of the patient (Case 3-B) who was pushed to marry a man she did not love by her mother. The problem in metacommunication was to find a way for the patient to bring up in an empathic way the issue of the mother's having done so. Bringing up the events leading up to the marriage was an important step in the patient's discussing her overall relationship with her mother; the goal was to significantly reduce the frequency and viciousness of the mother's criticism of her divorce.

The therapist theorized to the patient that the mother probably felt that she had done the patient a favor by pushing her into the marriage. The mother may have felt that she was protecting the patient by preventing her from following in the mother's footsteps, so to speak. If the patient were married to a nice young boy from a religious family, she would not run the risk of being attracted, as the mother had been, to a dangerous man like the patient's father. The patient was only half convinced by the therapist's theory; deep down she still believed that the mother's motivation was more sinister. The patient's theory was that the mother pushed her into the marriage in order to keep her under the mother's thumb. This view was reinforced by the mother's relentless criticism of her divorce, and the family's ongoing relationship with her exhusband.

The mother and daughter had of course been having disagreeable conversations about the divorce for many years. Because of this history, both the patient and the mother were always on high alert for negative characterizations of one by the other as soon as the subject was breached. In a conjoint session, the patient could not resist bringing up criticisms of the mother's behavior surrounding the marriage. She unexpectedly began to say something that implied that the mother did not have the patient's best interest at heart. In response, the mother went on the attack before the patient could even finish the sentence. The mother launched into another series of comments criticizing the patient for getting divorced—the very thing that the therapist wanted the patient to try to stop.

In discussing the conjoint session with the patient later, the therapist again suggested that the mother's impressive negativity could be explained by her feeling unappreciated for sacrifices she had made for the patient and unfairly blamed by the patient for the failure of the marriage. The patient had, in the mother's mind, destroyed what the mother thought to be a good situation. As the reader may recall, the patient had not really told her mother about the extent of the husband's neglect and devaluation of the patient. However, by this time the patient had become even more convinced that the mother only wanted to control her, and indicated an unwillingness to continue discussing ways to resolve the issue. Soon after this session, the patient's sibling, who had not yet been detriangulated, convinced her that she needed to see a different therapist.

STRATEGIES FOR INITIATING
METACOMMUNICATION

The patient's initial approach to the targeted other is usually critical in determining the success or failure of any given attempt at metacommunication. A successful start allows the patient to begin to describe ideas about the family dynamics to the target without encountering undue defensiveness or invalidation from the target. In turn, the discussion of family dynamics allows the patient to empathically discuss the nature and origins of difficulties in his or her own relationship with the target, and potential ways to improve it.

Unfortunately, a strategy that works wonderfully in one family may lead to disaster in another family that may superficially appear quite similar. Every family has it's own unique set of variables to which they overreact! There is usually no way to know in advance what the best opening will be. The therapist must find the best strategy through a trial-and-error process. The patient must be told explicitly in advance that such is the case. The therapist tells the patient in a matter-of-fact manner that he or she will be trying out a variety of ways to approach the other, and that some may work and some may not. It is necessary, in fact, to gain the patient's explicit verbal agreement not to try out any particular strategy until both he or she and the therapist have agreed on it, and the patient has had time to practice the strategy with the therapist.

Shortly, five general initial approaches are presented that can be tried out in a trial-and-error fashion during role reversal. After making an educated guess about which of the five strategies might work best with a given family member, the therapist should proceed with role playing. The therapist generally sticks with a given strategy even if the target's initial response is a negative one, such as evasive maneuver or a verbal invalidation of the patient. Such maneuvers can often be countered with specific responses that are employed as the conversation progresses; these are described after we review the initial strategies. If the therapist seems to get in trouble with escalating negativity from the targeted other even while employing the usual countermeasures, the therapist should stop the role playing and tell the patient that the particular approach being tried is probably not a good one. The therapist then tells the patient that he or she is going to try something else, and tries again with one of the other initial strategies.

If the usual approaches all seem inadequate, the therapist must use ingenuity to come up with other ways to counter specific interactional problem sequences. I have found that the best way to be ingenious is to just let my mind go wild and try anything that comes to mind. If nothing comes to mind and I am completely stumped, I admit it to the patient, and say, "I'm not sure how to handle that one; let me think about it between now and our next session." Between sessions, I will look over my process notes for clues as to what to do. If I am still unable to come up with a strategy that does not cause trouble, obtaining further information about the target's likely response pattern may become necessary. In this case, I tell the patient to test the waters, so to speak, by going to the target and trying out the first part of what seems to be the most promising of the so-far unsuccessful strategies. The patient is then told to quickly drop the subject with the target, and to write down an explicit description of the target's verbal and nonverbal reactions to the "test."

Of course, every time I am foolish enough to think that I have heard every possible negative response, I am surprised. In one instance, for example, a male patient's mother unexpectedly responded to an attempt at metacommunication by making a sexual overture to the patient!

The following are the five suggested initial strategies:

1.   The first option is to begin with a discussion of family history, using the core relationship problems as they were manifested in past generations as a metaphor for current interactional difficulties. The patient starts with nonthreatening questions about family history and then goes on to discuss more emotionally charged past family interactions that parallel the current problem. Next, the patient slowly traces with the target the history of the family problem into the present as it has come to affect the patient's current relationship with the target.

This strategy was the first one I devised and is discussed in more detail in a previous work (Allen, 1988). As the theory suggests, the current roles being played out by family members stem from issues that develop over at least three generations. Therefore, any problem in the present or in the patient's childhood has precedents in the interactions of the earlier generations. At this stage of therapy, the patient should already be aware of these precedents; they should have been incorporated into the therapist's interpretation of the family dynamics.

For families that do *not* produce individuals with BPD, strategy number one is often the least threatening option. It tends to be much less threatening for parents to discuss long-past relation-ship problems with their own parents, with their siblings (the patient's aunts and uncles), or even with the other parent than it is to discuss those very same problems as they exist with the patient in the here and now. The negative impact of the issues seems muted when viewed from the distant perspective of the past. However, once the analogous issues have been brought up for discussion, the patient can gradually demonstrate how the earlier difficulties have led to problems and miscommunication in the present. The patient can then say something like, "No wonder you reacted so strongly when I did [such and such]! I wish I knew that before. I always thought you reacted because [whatever explanation the patient had come up with prior to therapy]." During this process, the patient receives confirmation or clarification about the therapist's hypotheses regarding the family dynamics. In this scenario, the parents should feel that their child is really trying to understand them and not attack them.

Unfortunately, I have found that in families that produce offspring with BPD, strategy number one is often the worst option. In these families, the parents usually do not want to touch their feelings about their own families of origin with a 10-foot pole. There is so much repressed rage and anguish from the past that it is in fact easier for the patient and parents to talk about the here-and-now first. Rather than seeming distant, the past seems more alive in the present than it ever has. Even getting the target to describe interactions in previous generations for purposes of genogram data gathering and hypothesis generation can be extremely difficult. The parents do not want to think about their relationships in the past for fear of triggering an all-consuming emotional reaction. This leads us to strategy number two.

2. The second option is for the patient to cut to the chase and move directly into a tactful confrontation about how the target's current behavior affects the patient adversely. The term *confrontation* as I am using it once again means bringing up a problem for discussion, not picking a fight. If a direct confrontation is to succeed, there can be no sense whatever that the conversation is an adversarial proceeding. The patient must remain absolutely empathic and say nothing that even remotely suggests that the parents are to blame for his or her own problems. The best way to start

such a confrontation is to employ disclaimers. The use of disclaimers by the therapist with the patient was discussed in chapter 6; the patient uses them in exactly the same way with the target.

The opening gambit in this strategy is a statement such as "Dad, I know you always wanted me to succeed in my career, but when you did not come to my graduation, I began to wonder if somehow you might be threatened by my success." The patient is then coached to say nothing further and await some kind of response by the parent. Depending on how the target responds, the patient and target then go on to discuss how they have been misreading one another's intentions because of behavior they have both manifested that was due to each person's internal conflicts. The patient must be careful to acknowledge his or her own contribution to any misunderstanding while explaining that his or her behavior was due to a *misreading* of the target's motives. Such a conversation can lead to discussions of the past family history that has lead to the conflicts. If the target has a high level of emotionality about past interactions as mentioned previously, however, that part of the conversation must be approached with exceptional delicacy and tact.

3.   Initiation strategy number three is used in cases in which the patient has been sacrificing his or her idiosyncratic ambitions in order to overtly or covertly "look after" parents. Such patients may have been "on call" to help mediate the parents' disputes or provide missing companionship for a parent. Alternatively, in families with gender-role problems, an adult may live with a widowed mother so that either the mother appears to be dependent on her adult child or vice versa. The latter situation is created by the dyad in order to avoid the violation of any family proscriptions against women being powerful enough to make it on their own. In this situation, the adult child also appears to be in some way dysfunctional, so that the mother partially discharges her repressed ambition by running the adult child's life. In such cases, it is very difficult indeed to tell exactly who is taking care of whom.

The patient begins strategy number three with a statement that he or she is worried about the parent's well-being in some way. The patient might say, "I've been really worried about you, Mom. You've looked so lonely and depressed." The patient brings this up without any suggestions or advice about how Mom should take care of this problem. The reason for doing so is that the parent will usually argue with any particular advice offered by the patient—which is usually something fairly obvious anyway—in order to avoid dealing with his or her underlying loneliness and depression. As with the patient and the therapist, any such behavioral prescriptions that are offered by the patient can be dissected and debated ad infinitum, and the conversation invariably deteriorates into a game of "why don't you—yes but."

The initial response of the parent to the opening statement is usually something like, "You don't have to worry about me, I'm doing fine." Such statements are an invalidation of the patient's worries, because in most of these cases the parent really is depressed or lonely—or may be drinking too much or behaving self-destructively in some other way as the case may be. The statement is also an invalidation of the patient's caring and concern. The best response here is for the patient to say, "I appreciate the fact that you don't want me to trouble myself with your problems, but I really am concerned." Predictably, the parent will then respond with a distancing remark such as, "No you don't. You don't care about anyone but yourself." The patient can answer this type of statement in the same way the therapist would answer a similar accusation from a patient: "I wish I knew of a way to convince you that I really do."

In the case of a mother and, say, an adult son playing the game of "who is taking care of whom" described previously, the patient might begin strategy number three with a statement such as, "I know that you are perfectly capable of taking care of yourself, but sometimes you seem to be afraid to for some reason." With this opening gambit, the mother has an obvious comeback that she can use in order to avoid facing the dilemma that has been brought up—usually for the first time—by the patient. She can point out that it is really the patient who is the dependent one. After all, the patient has, up to that point, exhibited some apparent defect that has prevented him from going out an making his own life separate from Mom. In many of these cases Mom has bailed the son out of one financial bind after another. Who is he to be talking about the mother's dependency problem? In this situation, the patient is coached to confess that he has not striven for independence thus far, but that one of the reasons for his not having done so is his continued worry about how the mother might feel if left alone and on her own.

If the patient is successful at getting the parent to talk frankly about the patient's expressed areas of concern, the patient and target can then go on to discuss how they have been misreading one another's intentions and about the past family history that has lead to the problem. These topics are handled in much the same manner as described under strategy number two already discussed.

4. The fourth opening strategy is employed when mild to moderate distancing behavior by the parents is a primary obstacle to metacommunication. Distancing behavior is manifested when any attempt by the patient to get close to the parent or to discuss important family issues is met with hostility, verbal abuse, or other provocative behavior. The patient begins strategy number four by expressing a wish for more closeness with the parent. The patient says something like, "I really feel bad that we get along so poorly; I really wish that things were better between us."

This statement often leads to an initial positive reaction by the parent for two reasons. First, many distancing parents do not like to admit that their behavior is purposely designed to drive the patient away. In effect, they would have to do so if they were to blatantly reject this overture. Second, the statement appeals to the side of the parent's ambivalence that really does desire a close relationship with the patient. The patient's expressed desire for closeness in spite of the fact that the parents have been treating her or him horribly communicates such love for the parent that the parent's hostility often seems to melt away.

Unfortunately, in more severely disturbed families this type of approach may lead to an even nastier rejection of the patient than had been the norm previously. The parent may respond with a statement that communicates the sentiment, "Well, I do not want to be close to you; I wish you had never been born." If the patient playing the parent in a role-reversal exercise comes out with this kind of response, the therapist should be leery of coaching the patient to employ this strategy. The therapist can tell the patient that it is doubtful that the parent really feels that way even if he or she says it, but that some other strategy might work better. In some cases, however, the parent's nastiness is so transparently feigned that the patient can break through it by saying, "I don't believe that for a second."

If the parent responds to initiation strategy number four positively, patients are then coached to wonder aloud why they and the target are always fighting. This question can once again lead to empathic discussions of the nature and origins of mixed messages and misunderstandings within the relationship, which are in turn used as a basis for requesting concrete behavioral changes from the target.

5. The fifth opening gambit is useful in cases in which the patient is following in the parents' footsteps in some way. The patient recreates the parent's maladaptive behavior in order to shield the parents from feelings of envy. In these cases, the patient usually tries but fails to achieve some goal that is desperately desired by but forbidden to the parent. For example, a daughter might appear to seek out nice men but, just like her mother, end up with a succession of abusive mates. This may happen after the parent has spent years trying to shield the child from this very outcome or warning her about the dangers of it.

The patient begins strategy number five by asking the target for advice on how to handle a difficulty that the patient is experiencing outside of the patient's relationship with the target. The outside difficulty parallels a difficulty that the target has also experienced within the family. For example, in a family in which the patient's father always gives in to the mother's unreasonable demands, the daughter may come to the mother with the following request for help: "Mom, I need your advise. My husband is following me around like a puppy dog. How do you think I should handle it?"

The goal here is to establish a sense of commonality between the two women that allows for open discussion about how parallels in the family happened to have come about. Once again, this naturally leads to discussions of the nature and origins of mixed messages and misunderstandings within the relationship. In dysfunctional interactions, whenever one party brings up such parallels, the other party usually feels unjustly criticized, and therefore reacts negatively. This occurs for one of two reasons. First, the second party may feel that the first party is a hypocrite who is criticizing her for things the other party does herself. Alternately, one or the other party may feel that their situations, although similar, are not really the same at all.

Strategy number five changes the valence of the interaction from negative to positive in two ways. First, it puts the daughter in the proper hierarchy with the mother. The patient is asking the mother for advice based on the mother's experience and intelligence. Second, the mother usually does not feel criticized by the daughter for having the problem, because the daughter is admitting to having the same or similar problem herself.

All five initiation strategies, as well as any other creative approaches a therapist is able to devise, are meant to soften up the target, so to speak, so that the family dynamics can be discussed and clarified. As mentioned previously, if an initial approach that the therapist chooses seems promising, the role reversal exercise is continued to the point where the goal of the conversation is achieved. As the exercise continues, the therapist models interventions that the patient can employ to prevent the targeted other from derailing the metacommunication process. These interventions are the subject of the next section.

STRATEGIES FOR COUNTERING FAMILY BLOCKS TO METACOMMUNICATION

In families with a BPD member, members almost always have an armamentarium of tricks by which attempts at discussing sensitive issues by other family members can be thwarted. Many of these maneuvers take the form of comments that invalidate the offender in some way. During role playing, the therapist should be alert to invalidating comments made by the targeted other—as played by the patient—and employ a countermeasure designed to neutralize them. The appropriate countermeasures are thereby demonstrated and taught to the patient.

The countermeasures the therapist uses are exactly the same ones or very similar to those that the therapist employed with the patient at the beginning of therapy. In chapter 6, we discussed the multiple ways in which patients with BPD invalidate, disqualify, or frustrate the therapist, as well as ways for therapists to respond to them that lead the patient to become more cooperative. These actions by patients, in addition to being manifestations of each patient's false self, are also resistances to discussing sensitive issues with the therapist.

The patients probably learned these behavioral ploys in the first place from observing how their parents used the ploys on them. In a parallel fashion, the therapist teaches patients the countermeasures that had been used earlier on the patients by the therapist in order to break through resistances.

As mentioned, teaching the patient how to counter invalidation from the parent is done primarily through demonstration of the techniques in role reversal exercises. The techniques are then coached by the therapist and practiced by the patient during direct role playing. The reader can refer back to chapter 6 for a review of the techniques and how they should be used.

Besides invalidation, families of patients with BPD can employ a variety of other metacommunication-blocking techniques. Each of these techniques has a specific countermeasure that will usually thwart the target's attempt to derail the conversation. These measures and countermeasures were described in a previous work (Allen, 1988) and are described briefly here:

1. *Changing the Subject.* The target evades important issues by continually changing the subject to other important issues so that no single issue is ever covered in depth. Countermeasure: The patient insists on sticking to the subject. This is often best accomplished through statements such as, "We need to discuss that [new subject] further, but first let's finishing talking about [old subject]." This sort of statement communicates to the target that the patient recognizes the importance of subjects the target brings up, but keeps the conversation focused on one issue at a time.

2. *Making Fallacious Arguments.* The target may use a fallacious or illogical argument to derail metacommunication. The illogical argument is meant to confuse patients so that they become unsure of the point they are trying to make. Countermeasure: The patient tactfully expresses confusion about what the target is saying, or points out seeming contradictions. This is done in an almost apologetic fashion. Rather than accusing the other of purposely being misleading or confusing, patients try to indicate that they themselves are taking responsibility for any lack of interpersonal understanding. In response, the target often feels obliged to clear up the patients' confusion.

3. *Blame Shifting.* In blame shifting, the target tries to move the patient into a defensive stance by putting all the blame for the interpersonal difficulty on either the patient or a third party, while refusing to acknowledge in any way his or her own contribution. The discussion then deteriorates into a game of "who's to blame" instead of a discussion about how the problem can be avoided in the future.

   Countermeasures: If the patient is blamed, he or she acknowledges his or her own contribution to the problem. The patient then goes on to clarify that his or her behavior was based on a misunderstanding of what the other expected in the situation. An interesting example of this tact occurred in the case of a drug addicted BPD patient (Case 9-A) who was enmeshed in a relationship with her highly enabling mother. The mother constantly complained to the patient about what a financial burden the patient was yet would take care of her every need, often spending way more money on her than was necessary. Strangely, the mother would give the patient more money when the daughter did not ask for it than when she did. To add insult to injury, the mother would never acknowledge any instance in which the patient acted responsibly. The patient was coached to tell the mother about how bad she was feeling about all the financial problems the mother was having because of her. The mother predictably retorted that the patient could not really care about that because she was always badgering the mother for money. The patient then replied, "Yes, I do that, but part of the reason I do it is because you always seem so disappointed when I don't!"

   If third parties are blamed for a family problem, they are often attacked by the target in what appears to be an unfair manner. In this situation, patients normally tend to defend the other party, even if they are angry at that person themselves. This again leads to an argument about who is really to blame. Instead, the patient acknowledges the contributions of the other family members to the problem without criticizing their motives. Exaggerated characterizations of a third party are generally ignored.

4. *Fatalism.* In fatalism, the target tries to stop the conversation by declaring it useless. The statement usually takes the form of

"There's no way to change it, we should just accept it," or "Why dwell on the past?" Countermeasure: The patient is empathic with the target's fatalism, as he or she probably felt that same way prior to therapy. The patient replies, "I, too, used to think that you just had to accept these problems, but now I think there may be a way out."

5. *Nit Picking Over the Patient's Examples of Troublesome Interactions.* With this maneuver, the patient is drawn into an argument about the precise accuracy of any example of the problematic interaction that he or she tries to bring up. Countermeasure: The patient responds to the nit picking with, "Well perhaps that wasn't the best example, but I think you know what I'm talking about."

6. *Accusing the Patient of Overgeneralizing.* In this scenario, the target tells patients that the problematic interactions about which they are complaining do not arise nearly as often as they seem to think. The target will invariably offer counterexamples of times when the target or family members did not act in the way that the patient is suggesting. Countermeasure: Because the individuals in the BPD patient's family are highly conflicted, there will always be times when they seem to act in an atypical or even opposite way from the way they do most of the time. Therefore, the patient can agree with target's counterexample but reframe it as illustrating the family or the target's confusion and ambivalence over the issue in question.

7. *Walking Out.* The target simply stops the conversation cold and leaves the room in a huff. Countermeasure: Instead of pursuing the other into another room or giving up altogether, the patient temporarily abandons the attempt at metacommunication but tries again later at the first opportunity.

DETRIANGULATION STRATEGY

As mentioned earlier, when it becomes time for the patient to begin the process of metacommunication with the actual primary family members, it is usually necessary to first act to prevent other relatives from interfering. In this section we discuss how this is accomplished. As with all metacommunication, detriangulation strategies may need to be developed and tailored to the individual family member, and then practiced by the patient using role playing exercises. Again, the therapist starts with role reversal, and then has the patient practice the agreed-on strategy using direct role playing.

The basic detriangulation strategy consists of four tasks:

1. First, the patient informs the potential triangulator about the patient's plans to talk to the parental figures, and explains the justification for doing so. The patient explains the therapist's hypothesis about the family dynamics.

2. The patient then asks the triangulator what concerns he or she may have about the consequences of the patient's plan. These concerns often turn out to be nearly identical to the reservations that the patient had expressed to the therapist earlier on in therapy. For siblings and other relatives, the concerns usually center around a fear that the primary target will not be able to handle the confrontation, and may decompensate in some way, or that the confrontation may create tensions in other important dyadic relationships within the family. For a spouse or partner, concerns usually center around a fear that the patient will not get the hoped-for reaction from the salient figure and will then decompensate in some way. If the spouse has not been informed of the course of therapy all along as recommended, the spouse may also have concerns that any changes in the patient's role behavior will adversely affect the spouse's relationship with the spouse's own family of origin, and may feel betrayed.

3. Third, the patient reassures the triangulator about his or her concerns. The therapist coaches the patient to tell the triangulator that the patient has had similar concerns himself or herself, and that the patient and therapist have worked out a strategy that the patient believes will avoid any significant harm being done to anyone. The patient then describes the strategy. At times after this intervention, the potential triangulator may even make helpful suggestions about how the patient can refine the strategy.

4. Last, the patient makes the following type of statement to the triangulator: "I really think it would be best if I handled this myself, so I would appreciate if you did not talk to Mom about this before I have had a chance to do it. However, if you feel that

you must warn her or discuss with her the issues as they apply to you, then go ahead and do so."

The last sentence is a paradoxical statement designed to reduce the likelihood that the potential triangulator will go ahead and interfere. The statement appeals to the triangulator for cooperation while indicating that the patient will not be drawn into a power struggle about it. Many times, a sibling is already aware that the family behavior patterns are problematic in the way the patient describes, and becomes only too happy to let the patient try to take care of it. Furthermore, if the triangulator were to broach the taboo subject with the target, the initial negative reactions might fall on him or her. If the triangulator does go ahead and spill the beans, so to speak, the patient is in a better position to ask the target about what the triangulator said. Knowing this will help the patient better understand any negative reactions from the target that were set up by the triangulator's interference.

DIRECT ROLE PLAYING

Before asking the patient to actually confront significant others with any metacommunicative task, the therapist initiates role-playing exercises that allow the patient to try out and practice the strategies that the therapist has devised. After a strategy that seems to have a good chance of success has been devised during role reversal, the therapist changes roles with the patient. If the patient refuses to trade places, but expresses confidence that he or she can confront the significant other using the agreed-on strategy, and is able to demonstrate by verbal report understanding of the strategy and knowledge about potential difficulties, the therapist need not insist. However, practice during therapy is preferable. In cases in which the patient finds that, after approaching the target, he or she has difficulty sticking to the strategy, directly practicing it using role-playing exercises with the therapist becomes mandatory.

During direct role playing, the therapist should play the significant other as being as difficult and invalidating as possible, consistent with the known characteristics of the targeted other. For example, the therapist should use any "fighting words" (see chap. 4) that the target has used in the past that are particularly likely to inflame the patient. Presentation of worst-case scenarios is done for two reasons. First, should the worst case actually transpire, patients will be prepared for it. Second, the target usually does not react as badly as the therapist modeled in the role playing exercise. This eventuality leads patients to come away from their initial effort feeling more confident about both the strategy and their own ability to implement it.

The therapist gets "in character" by reviewing the hypothesis about the patient's specific family dynamics and attempting to identify issues about which the target is most likely to be sensitive. As previously discussed, parents of patients with BPD are generally hypersensitive to criticisms that even remotely suggest that they were bad parents or had evil intentions, especially if the parents have been abusive. They are most likely to react with fury if the patient does not clearly acknowledge his or her own role as spoiler and provocateur before discussing the parents' behavior. They are also very likely to have difficulty openly talking about their anger at their own parents. The therapist demonstrates defensive or other negative reactions by the target whenever the patient does not maintain empathy during the role play, or does not press on with the metacommunication strategy when the therapist, playing the target, reacts with distress.

The therapist should therefore be alert to blaming, attacking, or insensitive statements by the patient, and respond—while playing the other—in a negative way. The negative response should be consistent with the target's past behavior, which should have already have been described earlier in therapy by the patient or demonstrated during role reversal exercises. The goal of these techniques is to teach the patient to become aware of how she or he may subvert the strategy by reacting automatically in emotionally charged situations.

The therapist should check with the patient from time to time as to whether or not the therapist's portrayal of the targeted other is accurate. The therapist should directly ask patients if he or she is responding to the behavior portrayed by the patient during role playing in a way that is consistent with the target's usual tactics. Overt questioning may not be necessary, however, if the patient laughs and makes asides during the role playing such as "That's just what she would say!"

The therapist should persist with direct role playing until patients appear competent to confront the target and confident of their ability to do so, no matter what the target may throw back at them. In other words, the therapist should try to continue direct role playing until the patient maintains empathy, sticks to the strategy, and proceeds with persistence.

SUCCESSFUL METACOMMUNICATION:
CASE EXAMPLE

The following successful discussion between a patient and her mother about the mother's past history of severe physical abuse of the patient occurred in Case 4-C. Prior to the excerpt from the conversation, the patient had been having a long, drawn-out telephone conversation with the mother. In the course of a discussion of problems a sibling was having, an unexpected opportunity to bring up the abuse issue arose. The mother's words that provided the opportunity are underlined. The patient quickly seized the opportunity and tactfully and persistently pushed the issue. My comments about noteworthy aspects of the interchanges are provided in brackets and Italics. In the transcript, Pt is the patient and M is the mother:

Pt: … Until sis forms her own religion, don't worry about it.

M: She's got to find herself; that's for sure.

Pt: Yeah.

M: She has got to find herself. Right now she's just bouncing around.

Pt: I decided once I was going to change my religion.

M: *[The mother is probably engrossed in feeling guilty about the sister's problems, and does not hear the patient's last comment].* I told her one thing, though, "You better stop and <u>look back on the mistakes Mom made,</u> and remember, you have a little child there that you are responsible for.

Pt: [silent] *[The patient recognizes the opportunity—an admission by the mother of mistakes in child rearing—and steels herself].*

M: Well I thank God every day for all my children. *[These are fighting words, because the mother had not treated the children as if she were thankful for having them around].*

Pt: *[The patient holds her tongue and does not react to the fighting words].* She said something to me one night, the only night

we talked ... she said she thinks ... I don't remember how
she put it, but ... (pause) ... "The best thing in the world
that could have happened to my kids was us growing up
with you." Does that make sense?

M: [silence].

Pt: 'Cause we had some pretty hard times and she said it
would never happen with her kids. Then she went on to
tell me how she spanked her [child]! And I couldn't ... ah
... Mom, do you ever think about those days, and you ever
look back on 'em?

M: Yeah, I regret a lot of them *[Because the patient had brought
up "those days" in the context of a conversation about spanking
and "hard times," these words represent both an indirect admission that the abuse had taken place, and an indirect apology for
it. From this point in the conversation on, the events of the
abuse are never spelled out explicitly, but it is clear that both the
patient and the mother know exactly what is being discussed].*

Pt: Do you ever wonder why they happened?

M: No, but as I've gotten older I've been more able to see why.

Pt: Can you share it?

M: Well, it'd take too long over the phone. Sometime I will.
[The mother resists the invitation].

Pt: No, I'm paying this phone bill, this is mine. *[The patient is
persistent].*

M: No.

Pt: Well, some day I'd like you to. Maybe in a letter. Something I can keep. Maybe in a tape recording. I've always
wondered why. I'll tell you the reason I came up with.
*[The patient temporarily agrees to go along with the mother's
resistance, but then decides to continue the conversation by offering a theory she and the therapist had come up with. She
hopes this will cause the mother to feel obliged to comment on
the theory. It works].* You were never very happy with my
father. I don't know what your marriage was like in the
very beginning, but it seemed from [city] on, it was really
just the pits. Cause he was very violent, not just with us
but with you too. [The patient offers the theory about
why the mother was angry at the children]. Does that
make sense?

M: But I didn't. I didn't [Mother repeats the patient's theory]. *[The theory turns out to be wrong].*

Pt: *[Undeterred, the patient presses on].* But I didn't know that, and I was looking for reasons because I couldn't understand.

M: Sometimes I feel like it was cause of, um, um ... my only solution that I've come up with is that I felt like, there I was with four children, and I seemed to be in everybody's way. My children and I seemed to be in everybody's way. *[The mother overtly reveals her ambivalence about her children. From this point on, the mother goes on to explicate exactly why she felt "in the way," and how the feeling led to the abuse].*

IMPLEMENTING THE STRATEGY

After the direct role playing phase of therapy is complete, the therapist assigns as homework an actual confrontation with a targeted relative. The assignment of this homework involves three subtasks:

1. The patient and therapist set a time and place for the metacommunication to take place. This may involve helping the patient devise a strategy for getting the target alone in a somewhat private environment where the conversation can take place without distractions, and deciding the best time for the conversation to take place. Getting parents away from one another is an essential aspect of the metacommunication process. If the parents are highly enmeshed with each other, doing so may require a great deal of ingenuity.

2. The therapist instructs the patient to proceed with the interaction until the patient does not know how to continue, or until the target reacts negatively in a way that the patient can not counter, or until the goal of the conversation has been reached. The patient is instructed to, if stymied, beg off and withdraw by saying something like, "I'm not sure how to get this across; let me think about it so we can discuss it more later." The patient should be instructed to write down, at the conclusion of the conversation, everything that was said as closely to verbatim as possible, and return to therapy for further instructions.

3. Patients should be reassured that they can make no irreversible errors. If they lose their cool and say something cruel or blam-

ing, they can always go back and apologize for the way the earlier conversation turned out, without backing down from its main thrust.

When the patient returns for the session following the homework assignment, the therapist should inquire whether or not the homework conversation took place, and ask for a blow-by-blow account of everything that was said. If elements that had been incorporated into the assignment are missing from the patient's report (i.e., the patient does not mention addressing points that were rehearsed in role playing), the therapist must ask specifically if those points had been brought up. In cases involving confrontation of a parental figure over a primary relationship issue, the therapist can do so by reviewing the pertinent items from the following checklist:

1. When and in what environment was the relative confronted?
2. Which issues were discussed?
3. Did the patient communicate an understanding of the context of the target's behavior?
4. Did the patient acknowledge his or her own contribution, if any, to the problem?
5. Did the patient refer specifically to the target's ambivalence or mixed messages, and their effect on the patient?
6. Was there some sort of confirmation, overt or covert, from the target?
7. If there was abuse between patient and target, was there some expression of regret or apology from the target, directly or indirectly?
8. Did the patient avoid blaming?
9. Did the patient request some specific change in the relationship?

If the homework was not done, or only partially or incorrectly done, the therapist should explore with the patient the reasons why he or she was unable to do it, or was hesitant to do it. If the patient ran in to problematic reactions during the metacommunication process that he or she was unable to overcome, the therapist should try to figure out what might have gone wrong. Did the relative exhibit previously unidentified sensitivities? Did the patient make an accusatory or blaming statement?

If the therapist is able to identify the probable error, he or she offers the patient a hypothesis about why the problem took place and how it might be handled during the next attempt. The therapist explains, for example, in what way the targeted other may have misread the patient's comments, or felt blamed by them. A new strategy should then be devised. If necessary, role reversal may again be employed to redesign the strategy, followed by direct role playing to practice the newly refined procedure.

If the homework was a success, the therapist discusses with the patient what the next step will be. The therapist decides, with input from the patient, whether to bring up another issue with the same target, or go on to a different target, or move on to termination. The role reversal, direct role playing, and homework implementation processes are repeated for the next task. The therapist should generally stick with role playing and homework assignments until the patient has successfully confronted all primary figures about all primary and secondary issues, or until the patient elects, despite the therapist's efforts, to discontinue the process for whatever reason.

In cases in which all issues and figures have not been confronted, the therapist should continue to work with the patient's resistances or concerns until the patient adamantly refuses to go on. The patient may refuse because he or she believes enough has been done, or because anxiety over a particular issue or figure is too high. If the patient decides to stop the therapist can express concern that the therapy may turn out to be less effective than it might be if the patient were to proceed. Ultimately, of course, the patient makes the final decision regarding how far to go.

10

Termination

In this chapter, we review the procedures for bringing unified psychotherapy with BPD patients to a successful conclusion. The termination process involves a number of tasks. The patient may or may not need to work on developing new relationship habits or behavior patterns in the absence of the usual family reactions that had previously stymied those activities. The patient needs to be informed about what to expect in the future, and about how to react to relapses. Significant traps remain for the patient that must be addressed. The most dangerous of these in the termination phase of treatment is the phenomenon of post-individuation depression.

POST INDIVIDUATION DEPRESSION

Whenever patients with BPD start to develop more mature behavior patterns or react more assertively with parental figures, they paradoxically become more depressed. Masterson (1981) was the first to write extensively about this phenomenon. He referred to it as "post-individuation depression," and related it to the borderline triad described in Part I of this book. His theory predicts that patients beginning to self-actualize start to fear that their family, as represented by internalized objects, will abandon them, as has happened so frequently in the past. Therefore, they start to become depressed.

In unified therapy, I have found that, after patients have success-fully addressed major family patterns that have hitherto reinforced or triggered dysfunctional character traits or symptoms, they in-deed seem to become more depressed, and highly anxious as well. They do so even if their family, rather than abandoning them, starts to become very supportive of their new behavior. I believe this emo-tional reaction is indicative of the re-emergence of anomie or exis-tential groundlessness. While their old role behavior is no longer useful or desirable, patients have not yet had time to develop or practice new ways of relating to the world. Patients may begin to wonder anew who they really are, or feel hopelessly adrift. Further-more, they may start to mourn over all of the time they had previ-ously spent acting out self-destructive scripts, and come to the realization they have wasted a good portion of their lives.

This can be an extremely dangerous time for all concerned. For the patient, recurrences of previously controlled self-mutilation or other self-destructive behavior represent a significant risk. Worse still, the risk of a significant and serious suicide attempt may some-times rise to levels higher than at any previous time. Patients may think that, because they are feeling so bad, they are getting worse and that the therapist's strategy has failed. For therapists who do not recognized this phenomenon, the danger is that they might agree that the patient is worsening and begin to rethink their ther-apy strategy. They may even panic and resort to interventions that may undo some of the good that has been done. For the patient's family, the danger is that their reaction to the re-emergence of the pa-tient's affective symptoms and self-destructive behavior might lead them to fall back into old patterns of anxious overinvolvement. This in turn would feed into the patient's tendency to fall back into old patterns, thusly re-igniting the family process that created the prob-lem in the first place. This latter process is a variation on the "game without end," which is discussed later in the chapter.

The therapist's task is to watch for signs of post-individuation de-pression, particularly after the patient has successfully confronted family members. Whenever the patient is actually behaving in a more functional manner yet seems to become more disturbed or symptomatic, the therapist must address the issue. The most helpful thing that the therapist can do is to describe the clinical phenome-non of post-individuation depression to patients. The therapist can warn them that they may feel worse for a while, and then reassure them that the feelings are actually a sign that significant progress has been made, and that they will gradually go away as patients try out new behavior.

When patients hear that there is a name for the unnamed terror they are experiencing and that the therapist is familiar with it, they are more likely to find the therapist's remarks about the transitory nature of the feelings reassuring. I usually explain that whenever people get out of playing a role in their families that has been central to them for many years, it is natural for them to become even more uncertain about their identity and to feel overcome with fear about what the future may hold. This uncertainty, I add, is a very distressing experience. I empathize with the highly disturbing nature of this feeling, but add that its presence is evidence, paradoxically, that the patient is getting better. I encourage the patient to stay the course. I openly acknowledge that the patient only has my word on the subject to go on, but add that I have seen this phenomenon many times with other patients. The uncomfortable feelings have always passed in those other cases.

If the patient has been taking antidepressant or anti-anxiety medication, it is important that they stay on it during this time of transition. Occasionally it may become necessary to raise the dose temporarily. The therapist should inquire about suicidal ideation and about any old self-destructive behavior that may have re-emerged. If self-mutilation recurs, it is important that the therapist not overreact. The therapist should express concern about it but tell patients that this is probably just a temporary setback and is merely a reaction to having successfully altered their behavior patterns. The patient is then told that family members may react to the setback by reverting to old habits about which metacommunication has taken place. This last remark sets the stage for a psychoeducational discussion about the "game with end."

DISCUSSING THE "GAME WITHOUT END"
AND RELAPSES

The "game without end" (Watzlawick, Beavin, & Jackson, 1967) refers to a what takes place in any system of interacting individuals when one member requests a change in the rules by which the group has operated. This is precisely the situation that the patient who has been through the unified therapy process is in. Because the individuals that make up the group have been acting the same way for so long, it is natural for them to be suspicious of any such requests. If the patient had compulsively engaged in borderline behavior such as spoiling for years, how can anyone be sure he or she really wants to do, or is even capable of doing, something else?

I have described elsewhere (Allen, 1991) how successfully confronted family members will test a patient to see how serious he or she is about the requested change. This "test" often involves the tester ostensibly acceding to the patient's request for change, but doing so in a very obnoxious manner. If the patient then criticizes the tester, the tester starts to think that the patient really did not want the requested change in the first place. For example, a previously emotionally closed off husband may begin to share more of his feelings as the patient requested, but do so at an inopportune time. He may, for instance, state during a social gathering that he dislikes something the patient is doing in front of the patient's boss. If she tells him in so many words to shut up, he feels vindicated in his doubts about the sincerity of the wife's original request. The reasons people act in this way remain unclear.

The therapist should educate the patient about the game without end. The therapist informs the patient that such events are likely, and coaches the patient on how to handle this type of problem should it arise or if it has already arisen. Generally, the strategy is for the patient to first praise the relative for attempting to do as the patient has requested before going on to quibble about the manner in which the attempt was made. The patient is coached to make a statement such as, "I'm very glad that you're starting to tell me how you feel, but it's hard for me to listen if you do it in front of my boss." The goal is to help the couple avoid falling quickly into old patterns due to the game without end phenomenon.

Relapse of family behavior is a phenomenon that may have effects similar to those of the game without end. Old, well-ingrained habits die hard. Sooner or later, no matter how hard they try to act differently, family members are bound to make mistakes and fall back into old patterns. This is inevitable and predictable, but when it happens, the danger is that the relapsed behavior may trigger an old *response* pattern from the rest of the family. The family may experience this in much the same way as they experience a game without end, and the gains the family has made may begin to unravel.

As with the game without end, the therapist should educate patients about what to expect in the way of relapses of old behavior patterns, and coach them on how to handle them. The recommended intervention is very similar to the paradoxical therapy technique (Weeks & L'Abate, 1982) of predicting relapses, and may in fact reduce the likelihood of relapse somewhat. Nonetheless, the therapist's prediction of relapse is not merely a strategy but is an accurate statement about what is very likely to happen.

The therapist briefly mentions to the patient that old habits are hard to break, so those old patterns of behavior may recur from time to time. However, the patient should not panic if it looks as if family members have moved back to square one. He or she now has enough skills to recognize such occurrences and put a stop to them. All the patient has to do is to wait until the family member cools down, and then bring up the incident, without blaming any one in particular, as an example of the type of behavior they had already discussed. The patient can then go on to tactfully remind the family member about how they had decided to try to change these types of interchanges.

ENCOURAGING THE PATIENT TO EXPERIMENT WITH NEW BEHAVIOR PATTERNS AND NEW TYPES OF RELATIONSHIPS

A good many patients who are in or have completed the process of metacommunication with central family members about the family dynamics spontaneously begin to experiment with healthy activities that were fearfully avoided in the past. They may start looking for a better job, attending parties, or dating nonabusive men. Other patients, however, may need a gentle push from the therapist to start doing so. Still others have developed a severe conditioned-anxiety response to healthy behavior, and may require further help from the therapist in extinguishing this anxiety.

In cases in which the patient does not spontaneously begin to try out new lifestyles, the therapist should first use gentle encouragement to get the patient to try out new behavior. It is often useful to obtain the patient's commitment to do a particular activity by a certain date. For those patients who had gravitated to destructive romantic relationships and are now unattached, the therapist can advise the patient to date a variety of types of people prior to getting involved with any one of them.

In cases in which old conditioned fears remain, but family reinforcement of old patterns is no longer a factor, the therapist may have to work with the patient to overcome the anxiety or do some brief social-skills training. This can be done using traditional cognitive-behavioral techniques. At this point in therapy, these techniques usually work surprisingly quickly, easily, and effectively. The reason for this is that, because of the change in family response patterns, the powerful effects of family invalidation are no longer actively undermining them.

ENDING THERAPY

Therapy should be terminated soon after the patient has finished confronting the central relatives about each central issue, and the patient has started to experiment with more healthy behavior. Therapists communicate to the patient that they now have confidence that the patient has the requisite skills for handling troublesome family interactions, so that he or she can now lead a more productive life. The therapist exhibits faith that the patient has had the abilities, strength, and intelligence to be successful in life all along, but had not been able to express these qualities previously for fear of the consequences.

There are no hard and fast rules about whether or not session frequency should be gradually tapered off. This can be left up to the individual patient and therapist to decide. The therapist should not drag the process out too long, however, lest the patient think that the therapist doubts that the patient can survive without the therapist.

In the last session, therapists should praise the patient for the patient's efforts in therapy without discounting their own contribution. This should be done even if the patient has only completed part of the therapist's "solution" and has decided not to proceed further. The therapist can make the following type of statement: "I've really been impressed by the way that you've taken what we've talked about and put it to good use."

It is often helpful to arrange a follow-up evaluation 4 to 6 months after termination, to see if the patient and family have begun to relapse. Finally, the therapist expresses confidence that the patients will not need to come back to treatment, but tells them they are welcome to do so if they feel the need.

References

Akiskal, H., Chen, E., Davis, G., Puzantan, V., Kashgarian, M., & Bolinger, S. (1985). Borderline: An adjective in search of a noun. *Journal of Clinical Psychiatry, 46,* 41–48.

Allen, D. (1988). *A family systems approach to individual psychotherapy* (originally titled *Unifying Individual and Family Therapies*). Northvale, NJ: Jason Aronson.

Allen, D. (1991). *Deciphering motivation in psychotherapy.* New York: Plenum.

Allen, D. (1993). Unified therapy. In G. Stricker & J. Gold (Eds.), *Comprehensive handbook of psychotherapy integration* (pp. 125–137). New York: Plenum.

Allen, D. (1997). Techniques for reducing therapy-interfering behavior in patients with borderline personality disorder: Similarities in four diverse treatment paradigms. *Journal of Psychotherapy Practice and Research, 6*(1), 25–35.

Allen, D. (2001). Integrating individual and family systems psychotherapy to treat borderline personality disorder. *Journal of Psychotherapy Integration, 11*(3), 313–331.

Allen, D., & Farmer, R. (1996). Family relationships of adults with borderline personality disorder. *Comprehensive Psychiatry, 37,* 43–51.

American Psychiatric Association. (1994). *Diagnostic and statistical manual of mental disorders* (4th ed.). Washington, DC: Author.

Barrett, M., & Trepper, T. (1992). Unmasking the incestuous family. *The Family Therapy Networker,* May–June, 39–46.

Benjamin, L. (1993). *Interpersonal diagnosis and treatment of personality disorders.* New York: The Guilford Press.

Berne, E. (1964). *Games people play.* New York: Grove Press.

Bezirganian, S., Cohen, P., & Brook, S. (1993). The impact of mother–child interaction on the development of borderline personality disorder. *American Journal of Psychiatry, 150,* 1836–1842.

Boszormenyi-Nagy, I., & Krasner, B. (1986). *Between give and take: A clinical guide to contextual therapy.* New York: Brunner/Mazel.

Bowen, M. (1978). *Family therapy in clinical practice*. New York: Jason Aronson.

Bowlby, J. (1988). Developmental psychiatry comes of age. *American Journal of Psychiatry, 145*, 1–10.

Bradley, S. (1979). Relation of early maternal separation to borderline personality in children and adolescents: A pilot study. *American Journal of Psychiatry, 136*, 424–426.

Brandchaff, B., Stolorow, R., & Atwood, G. (1992). Treatment of borderline states: An intersubjective approach. In D. Silver & M. Rosenbluth (Eds.), *Handbook of borderline disorders* (pp. 121–154). Madison: International University Press.

Brothers, L. (1997). *Friday's footprint*. New York: Oxford University Press.

Coccaro, E., & Kavoussi, R. (1997). Fluoxetine and impulsive aggressive behavior in personality-disordered subjects. *Archives of General Psychiatry, 54*, 1081–1088.

Conterio, K., & Lader, W. (1998). *Bodily harm*. New York: Hyperion.

Dawson, D. (1988). Treatment of the borderline patient, relationship management. *Canadian Journal of Psychiatry, 33*, 370–374.

Dawson, D., & Macmillan, H. (1993). *Relationship management of the borderline patient: From treatment to understanding*. New York: Brunner/Mazel.

DeShazer, D. (1988). *Clues: Investigating solutions in brief therapy*. New York: W. W. Norton & Company.

Donaldson, S., & Westerman, M. (1986). Development of children's understanding of ambivalence and causal theories of emotions. *Developmental Psychology, 22*(5), 655–662.

Edelman, G. (1989). *The remembered present: A biological theory of consciousness*. New York: Basic Books.

Eissler, K. R. (1953). The effect of the structure of the ego on psychoanalytic technique. *Journal of the American Psychoanalytic Association, 1*, 104–143.

Everett, C., Halperin, S., Volgy, S., & Wissler, A. (1989). *Treating the borderline family: A systemic approach*. Boston: Allyn and Bacon.

Frank, H., & Paris, J. (1981). Recollections of family experience in borderline patients. *Archives of General Psychiatry, 38*, 1031–1034.

Ginsburg, H., & Opper, S. (1969). *Piaget's theory of intellectual development*. Englewood, NJ: Prentice Hall.

Gold, J., & Wachtel, P. (1993). Cyclical psychodynamics. In G. Stricker & J. Gold (Eds.), *Comprehensive handbook of psychotherapy integration* (pp. 59–72). New York: Plenum Publishers.

Goldberg, R., Mann, L., Wise, T., & Segall, E. (1985). Parental qualities as perceived by borderline personality disorders. *Hillside Journal of Clinical Psychiatry, 7*, 134–140.

Greenberg, L., Rice, L., & Elliot, R. (1993). *Facilitating emotional change*. New York: Guilford.

Gunderson, J., Kerr, J., & Englund, D. (1980). The families of borderlines: A comparative study. *Archives of General Psychiatry, 37*, 27–33.

Gunderson, J., & Sabo, A. (1993). The phenomenological interface between borderline personality disorder and PTSD. *American Journal of Psychiatry, 150*, 19–25.

Gustafson, J. (1986). *The complex secret of brief psychotherapy.* New York: W. W. Norton & Company.

Harter, S. (1986). Cognitive-developmental processes in the integration of concepts about emotions and the self. *Social Cognition, 4*(2), 119–151.

Herman, J., Perry, J., & van der Kolk, B. (1989). Childhood trauma in borderline personality disorder. *American Journal of Psychiatry, 146,* 490–495.

Hoffman, P., Fruzetti, A., & Swenson, C. (1999). Family Treatment in Dialectical Behavior Therapy. *Family Process, 38*(4), 399–414.

Horowitz, M. (1988). *Introduction to psychodynamics: A new synthesis.* New York: Basic Books.

Ivey, A. (1986). *Developmental therapy.* San Francisco: Jossey-Bass.

Kernberg, O. (1994). Aggression, trauma, and hatred in the treatment of borderline patients. *The Psychiatric Clinics of North America, 7,* 701–714.

Kerr, M., & Bowen, M. (1988). *Family evaluation.* New York: W. W. Norton & Company.

Kohut, H. (1971). *The analysis of the self.* New York: International Universities Press.

Kohut, H. (1977). *The restoration of the self.* New York: International Universities Press.

Linehan, M. (1993). *Cognitive behavioral treatment of borderline personality disorder.* New York: Guilford.

Links, P., & Munroe-Blum, H. (1990). Family environment and borderline personality disorder: Development of etiologic models. In P. Links (Ed.), *Family environment and borderline personality disorder* (pp. 1–24). Washington, DC: American Psychiatric Press.

Links, P., Steiner, M., & Offord, D. (1988). Characteristics of borderline personality disorder: A Canadian study. *Canadian Journal of Psychiatry, 33,* 336–340.

Livesay, W. J. (2000). A practical approach to the treatment of patients with borderline personality disorder. *Psychiatric Clinics of North America, 231,* 211–232.

Livesay, W., Jang, K., Jackson, D. N., & Vernon, P. (1993). Genetic and environmental contributions to dimensions of personality disorders. *American Journal of Psychiatry, 150,* 1826–1831.

Luborsky, L., & Crits-Christoph, P. (1990). *Understanding transference: The CCRT method.* New York: Basic Books.

Masterson, J. (1981). *The narcissistic and borderline disorders: An integrated developmental approach.* New York: Brunner/Mazel.

McGoldrick, M., & Gerson, R. (1985). *Genograms in family assessment.* New York: W. W. Norton & Company.

Melges, F., & Swartz, M. (1989). Oscillations of attachment in borderline personality disorder. *American Journal of Psychiatry, 146,* 1115–1120.

Millon, T. (1987). On the genesis and prevalence of the borderline personality disorder: A social learning thesis. *Journal of Personality Disorders, 1*(4), 354–372.

Mosak, H. (1989). Adlerian psychotherapy. In R. Corsini & D. Wedding (Eds.), *Current psychotherapies* (4th ed., pp. 65–116). Itasca, IL: F. E. Peacock Publishers, Inc.

Ogata, S., Silk, K., Goodrich, S., Lohr, N., Westen, D., & Hill, E. (1990). Childhood sexual and physical abuse in adult patients with borderline personality disorder. *American Journal of Psychiatry, 147,* 1008–1013.

Palazzoli, M., Boscolo, L., Cecchin, G., & Prata, G. (1978). *Paradox and counterparadox.* New York: Jason Aronson.

Paris, J. (1993). Introduction. In J. Paris (Ed.), *Borderline personality disorder: Etiology and treatment* (pp. 3–12). Washington, DC: American Psychiatric Press.

Paris, J. (1998). *Working with traits: Psychotherapy of personality disorders.* Northvale, NJ: Jason Aronson.

Scheel, K. (2000). The empirical basis of dialectical behavior therapy: Summary, critique, and implications. *Clinical Psychology: Science and Practice, 7,* 68–86.

Selman, R. (1980). *The growth of interpersonal understanding.* San Diego: Academic Press.

Shapiro, E. (1978). Research on family dynamics: Clinical implications for the family of the borderline adolescent. *Adolescent Psychiatry, 6,* 360–376.

Shapiro, E. (1982). The holding environment and family therapy with acting out adolescents. *International Journal of Psychoanalytic Psychotherapy, 9,* 209–226.

Shapiro, E. (1992). Family dynamics and borderline personality. In D. Silver & M. Rosenbluth (Eds.), *Handbook of borderline disorders* (pp. 471–493). Madison, WI: International University Press.

Shapiro, E., & Freedman, J. (1987). Family dynamics of adolescent suicide. *Adolescent Psychiatry, 14,* 191–207.

Siegel, D. (1999). *The developing mind: Toward a neurobiology of interpersonal experience.* New York: The Guilford Press.

Sifneos, P. (1992). *Short term anxiety provoking psychotherapy: A treatment manual.* New York: Basic Books.

Slipp, S. (1984). *Object relations: A dynamic bridge between individual and family treatment.* New York: Jason Aronson.

Snyder, S., Pitts, W., Goodpaster, W., & Gustin, Q. (1984). Family structure as recalled by borderline patients. *Psychopathology, 17,* 90–97.

Soloff, P., & Millward, J. (1983). Developmental histories of borderline patients. *Comprehensive Psychiatry, 24,* 547–588.

Steiner, C. (1971). *Games Alcoholics Play.* New York: Ballantine.

Symonds, A., & Symonds, M. (1985). Karen Horney. In H. Kaplan & B. Saddock (Eds.), *Comprehensive textbook of psychiatry IV* (pp. 419–426). Baltimore: Williams & Wilkins.

Tyler, S. (1978). *The said and the unsaid.* New York: Academic Press.

Van Reekum, R. (1993). Acquired and developmental brain dysfunction in borderline personality. *Canadian Journal of Psychiatry, 38* (February Supplement), S4–S10.

Walsh, F. (1977). Family study 1976: 14 borderline cases. In R. Grinker & B. Werble (Eds.), *The borderline patient* (pp. 158–177). New York: Jason Aronson.

Watzlawick, P., Beavin, J., & Jackson, D. D. (1967). *Pragmatics of Human Communication.* New York: W. W. Norton & Company.

Weeks, G., & L'Abate, L. (1982). *Paradoxical psychotherapy: Theory and practice with individuals, couples, and families.* New York: Brunner/Mazel.

Westen, D. (1991). Social cognition and object relations. *Psychological Bulletin, 109*(3), 429–455.

Wilson, E. (1998). *Consilience: The unity of knowledge.* New York: Alfred A. Knopf.

Yeomans, F., Selzer, M., & Clarkin, J. (1992). *Treating the borderline patient: A contract-based approach.* New York: Basic Books.

Zanarini, M., & Frankenburg, F. (1994). Emotional hypochondriasis, hyperbole, and the borderline patient. *Journal of Psychotherapy Practice and Research, 3,* 25–36.

Zanarini, M., Gunderson, J., Marino, M., Schwartz, E., & Frankenburg, F. (1989). Childhood experiences of borderline patients. *Comprehensive Psychiatry, 30,* 18–25.

Author Index

A

Akiskal, H., 5
American Psychiatric Association, 27, 92
Atwood, G., 9

B

Barrett, M., 79
Beaven. J., 188
Benjamin, L., 6, 12, 20, 26, 29, 38
Berne, E., 137
Berzerganian, S., 6
Bolinger, S., 5
Boscolo, L., 20
Boszormenyi-Nagy, I., 77
Bowen, M., 16, 28, 160
Bowlby, J., 25
Bradley, S., 5
Brandchaft, B., 9
Brook, S., 6
Brothers, L., 14

C

Cecchin, G., 20
Chen, E., 5
Clarkin, J., 89
Cocarro, E., 108
Cohen, P., 6
Conterio, K., 111
Crits-Cristoph, P., 37, 131

D

Davis, G., 5
Dawson, D., 110
De Shazir, D., 137
Donaldson, S., 23

E

Edelman, G., 135
Eissler, K. R., 87
Elliot, R., 131
Englund, D., 5
Everett, C., 11

F

Farmer, R., 3, 26
Frank, H., 5
Frankenburg, F., 3, 5
Freedman, J., 6
Fruzetti, A., 77

G

Gerson, R., 38
Ginsburg, H., 23
Gold, J., 16, 20
Goldberg, R., 5
Goodrich, S., 3
Goodpasteur, W., 5
Greenburg, L., 131
Gunderson, J., 3, 5

Subject Index

A

Abandonment issues, 28, 186–187
Abuse, *see also* Child abuse, Child
    neglect
    physical, 3, 31, 58
    sexual, 3, 5, 31, 38, 57–58
    verbal, 31, 172
Accepting patient's reactions, 125–126
Accommodation, 22, 88
Accusations, wild, 96–97, 101
Adler, Alfred, 137
Adlerian question, 134, 137–141
Affect regulation, 72–73, 110–111
Affective disorders, 31
Alcoholics Anonymous, 20
Alcoholic husband and nagging wife,
    17–18
Altruism, 14–16, 76
    hidden, 16–17, 93
Ambiguity, 51, 56, 60
    motivational, 131
Ambivalence
    as cause of atypical family behavior,
        177
    development of concept in children
        of, 23
    focusing on during therapy, 141–142
    in homework assignments, discus-
        sion of, 147, 184
    and metacommunication failure,
        50–52

and parental role confusion, 37–40
in repetitive negative interactions,
    19–20
about therapist's response pattern,
    85
in the spouse, 128
Anomie, *see,* Anxiety, existential
Anticonvulsants, 108
Antidepressants, 97, 105, 188
    in post-individuation depression,
        188
    mono amine oxidase inhibitors
        (MAOI's), 107
    selective serotonin reuptake inhibi-
        tors (SSRI's), 107–109
    tricyclic, 107
Antisocial traits, 33, 65
Antithetical meanings, in human com-
    munication, 51
Anxiety disorders, 31, 105
Anxiety, existential, 17, 29–30, 68, 74,
    138, 162, 186
Anxiety provoking technique, 125
Apology
    patient, 164, 184
    therapist, 102
Apparent competence, 13, 30
Arguments, irrational patient, 98
"Asking for it," 9, 18–19, 60, 94
Assertiveness skills, 78, 162
Assimilation, 22, 82
Attachment theory, 6